Your *Life* *as a* *River*

REFLECTING ON THE **PAST** TO CREATE A **STRENGTHS** BASED FUTURE

DR. THERESE LASK

To Jeff and Alec, my one thing.

Contents

Introduction

We have all had times in our lives when we needed to find the strength to navigate a path through difficulties. And, fortunately, we are usually able to do it. But where does that strength come from? How are we able to call on it to help us deal with those kinds of situations? And perhaps most important, can we draw on it to help us achieve our potential in other areas of our lives? The answer to these questions is essentially what this book is about.

I discovered these strengths in the process of preparing my doctoral dissertation on the pre-collegiate and collegiate experiences of first-generation college students. As a first-generation college student myself, I had always been aware of how difficult a journey people like me had to face. But in my role as Director of Student Support Services at Aims Community College, I was struck by how much more difficult it is today than it was even for those of my generation. Despite the increased importance of getting a college education, the obstacles to doing so can be almost overwhelming, particularly for students in substandard educational systems that fail to enable them to even dream of enrolling in college.

My study was designed to provide the voices of these students—and their stories —for those interested in researching the subject. I had just completed a series of student interviews when, through Dr. Idahlynn Karre of the Chair Academy, I learned about the Strengths Movement and the work of Dr. Donald Clifton and the Gallup Organization. Having completed the Strengths Finder assessment myself, I became aware for the first time of behaviors that I had exhibited my whole life, and at Dr. Karre's suggestion, I began looking at the data I had gathered for my dissertation from a strengths perspective. When I did, the stories I had collected took on an entirely new meaning.

In order to determine the extent to which these students' strengths had helped them navigate their pre-collegiate and collegiate experiences, I had seven of those I'd interviewed take the Strengths Finder assessment approximately six months after I had conducted my interviews. When they reported the results of their assessments I wasn't sure that I would find any connection between their strengths and their life stories. However, when I re-examined their stories, it became very clear that all seven of the students had made use of their strengths, in good times and bad, to navigate their lives. I subsequently asked two additional students, Kimberly and Susan, to be interviewed for this book, and to take the Strengths Finder assessment. And when I reviewed the results of their assessments in light of their life stories, it was clear that they had also made extensive use of their strengths at various times in their lives. Most important, I realized that the way they did so provided a roadmap that we can all use to make the most of our individual potential.

This book, then, explores how drawing on our strengths can contribute to every aspect of our lives. Toward that end, Chapters One and Two present a foundation for the concepts outlined in the book. The first presents an overview of the concepts of talents and shows how those talents, combined with knowledge and skill, can be developed into strengths. The second examines four key concepts in the use of our talents, including our combination of talents, the balcony and basement use of our talents, the importance of our key relationships and how they impact and are impacted on by our talents, and how our talents help us get through the difficult times in our lives. Chapters Three through Eleven present the stories of the nine first-generation college students I interviewed and their educational journeys. Although these nine individuals differed in age and life experiences, they all demonstrated how their unique combination of talents impacted on their life journeys, both for good and ill. Particularly poignant are the turning points they all experienced, the moments in time that lead them to enroll in a local community college in an effort to create a better life for themselves and for those they loved. It also provides you with a means of examining your own strengths by reviewing your life journey, as well as showing how you can use them to build a strength-based life and become all that you can be.

No RIVER can return to its source,
yet all RIVERS must have a BEGINNING

–NATIVE AMERICAN PROVERB

CHAPTER ONE

The Analogy of the River

*I*t begins with just a few drops of water dripping down an embankment from a mountain lake. But as the drops increase in number, the path they cut in the soft earth grows wider until the flow becomes a small stream. A little further on, the stream is joined by another stream, then another, and yet another, gaining in size, strength, and speed until it's no longer just a trickle of water but a powerful force carving its way through the landscape. Sometimes the water is tranquil, moving so slowly that it's easy to cross, while at other times it moves much faster, so fast that it's impossible to get to the other side. And as it flows, it takes on a life of its own, twisting and turning, going first in one direction and then another. The river has a destination—the sea—but until it reaches that destination it will twist and turn a thousand different times and in a thousand different ways.

Now imagine your life as a river. Like a river, you begin small, then change in size and strength as you grow. Also like a river, your life has in all likelihood been turbulent at times and calm and peaceful at others. It also probably hasn't flowed in just one direction but, instead, has taken numerous twists and turns, maybe so many that at times you've lost track of where you are going. Just as a river is joined by other streams, your life has been joined by family, friends, and others who have had an impact on you and on the direction in which you've traveled. Finally, just as a river moves towards its destination, so too does your life.

What is it, though, than enables you to navigate the river that is your life? What is it that makes it possible for you to make your way through rapids and calm waters, through turbulent times and peaceful ones? Ultimately, it is the innate talents that every one of us has. It is these talents, and the growth and development of these talents, that provide us with the opportunity to become the best versions of ourselves, the kind of people who can not only handle all that life offers but also benefit from the experience. We have all used these talents in the past to varying degrees of success. At times we have tapped into our talents in such a way that we were able to glimpse excellence, a standard of success we had no idea could be achieved. At other times we've used our talents in situations leading to our own detriment, getting in the way of our goals and aspirations. Most important, though, is that how we've used our talents provides each one of us with a key to our future. This book is about how we've used those talents at different points in our lives and how we can make use of them in the future to reach our greatest potential.

Of course, each of us has his or her own life, and no one's is exactly the same as anyone else's. So if, or example, you were to ask three people to draw their lives as a river, they would all draw very different pictures. One, for example, might draw his life as a river that meanders wildly and is filled with rocks that impede the current along the way. The rocks, in this case, might symbolize the challenges he's faced in selecting a college, a major, and a career, and the turns represent instances in which he put his talents to use to meet those challenges. A second person might draw a river that has fewer dramatic twists and turns but that flows great distances. For her, having moved frequently from one place to another as she grew up, these distances represent how she used her talents to adjust from one place to another. The final person might draw a river with sharp, dramatic drops, illustrated with short, dark strokes of the marker, reflecting a painful childhood during which she was forbidden from tapping into her talents. Although all of these stories are different, in each one the river provides a picture of how these individuals used their talents in good and bad times to navigate their lives.

WHAT ARE TALENTS?

Our talents are the essence of who we truly are, but exactly what are talents? Talents can be defined as natural, reoccurring patterns of thoughts, feelings or behaviors (Clifton, Anderson and Schreiner 2006, 2). We are often unable to define exactly what they are, or why we possess them, but we know that they are real, and that they provide a foundation for our lives. Not only do we all possess such talents, each of us also tends to have some talents that predominate over others. Predominant talents are those we use on a regular basis, with frequency and great ease, and we begin to exhibit them in childhood. For example, at an early age, some children demonstrate a fierce competitive spirit, striving to win first place in any competition. Some show a strong sense of discipline, and seek structure and order in every activity in which they're involved. And others strive to quickly turn their thoughts into actions. The point is that each of us possesses unique talents that draw us to certain activities and situations where we can utilize those patterns of thoughts, feelings or behaviors.

In fact, it's during childhood that we all start being drawn to such activities. For example, children with a keen competitive need will seek out any activity where they can compare themselves to others. Those with strong discipline will gravitate towards environments in which there is an established routine, where the same activities take place at the same time every day. And those who like to turn their thoughts into action will think of a new game and try it out almost immediately. But we don't always use our talents to our benefit. While we can and do start to develop healthy strategies in childhood, we also sometimes do things that can stifle our potential for personal growth and development. For example, the child with a keen competitive nature may start to do anything to win, even if it's unfair. A child with a penchant for discipline may take it too far by becoming frustrated when activities lack a certain amount of structure and order. And the child who is anxious to put thoughts into actions may do so without given sufficient consideration to the possible consequences.

Regardless of whether we develop positive or negative strategies as young children, once we enter school we invariably begin to lose track of our talents, and are unable to place ourselves in activities and relationships in which we can utilize our gifts. This is largely because as soon as we start school we are expected to perform certain activities in specific ways, rather than being allowed the opportunity to approach tasks using our unique set of talents. In other words, we are essentially forced to fit into the structured environment of school, where only certain talents are encouraged and others are ignored. As a result, children who are particularly comfortable with routine and structure often find school a perfect fit, because they are able to utilize this talent on a daily basis in the classroom. On the other hand, children who would prefer spending more time on lessons that pique their interest can be frustrated by being forced to move from one activity to another.

Moving on to college, however, can provide us with the opportunity to use and development our talents again, because in college we can choose to pursue studies in fields that are linked to our unique patterns of thoughts, feelings or behaviors. For example, students who are interested in cultivating the potential of others might major in fields that lead to the various helping professions, such as psychology, human services, and counseling. Those who tend to be more analytical, and are likely to seek reasons and causes in various situations, might go into the sciences, including biology, chemistry, and physics. Unfortunately, though, too few students pursue majors and career paths that complement their talents. This is because they've often had little or no guidance on how to link their talents to their course of study. As a result, many students graduate without understanding how, or even that, they can use their talents to achieve their greatest potential.

As we enter the workforce, the challenge of matching our talents to a future career becomes even more difficult. This is primarily because we are often unable to verbalize what our unique talents are or how we use them. There is, of course, a small percentage of individuals who graduate with a keen sense of their talents, and for them the workplace can provide a great sense of fulfillment and satisfaction. Not only do they feel energized and challenged, they also achieve a greater level of success. Most of us, however, do not experience that level of career fulfillment, satisfaction, and success, and while this is in part due to the nature of the workplace, we also have to take responsibility for it ourselves. Organizations almost invariably hire people on the basis of structured job descriptions, and rarely have the flexibility to adjust those descriptions to capitalize on an individual's unique talents. At the same time, when we lack the understanding of how to make the best use our talents, we are unable to seek out positions that provide the opportunity to best nurture those talents. As a result, many of us spend our time working at jobs that are frustrating and boring rather than in positions that allow us to develop our talents toward our greatest potential.

Our talents are not, however, just about our education and careers. They are also about how we live our lives. If you were to draw a picture of your life as a river, your education and career path would certainly be important components, but only of a much larger, more complex picture. Your picture would also show relationships with the people who have impacted on your life, your personal goals, times when you overcame difficulties, and times when you celebrated great events, like getting married or having a child. All of these things are important parts of your life, and even though you may not be aware of it, every one of them is affected by, and impacted on, by your talents. How does this work, and how, using the past as a guide, can we intentionally use our talents to achieve our greatest potential? One answer has been provided by what has come to be called the Strengths Movement.

THE STRENGTHS MOVEMENT

Since the early days of modern psychology, many practitioners have believed that if we could "fix" certain human behaviors we would be able to grow and develop to our greatest potential. The psychological self-help industry emerged from this belief, bringing forth an avalanche of ideas on how we can improve ourselves. If you walk into any bookstore you will find a section dedicated to improving our relationships, our work, and virtually every other aspect of our lives. We are a society dedicated to fixing ourselves. But beginning in the 1960s, a different perspective emerged in the field, one that offered a paradigm shift, a change in ideas. Instead of focusing on what was wrong with our behavior, it focused on what was right. The positive psychology movement was born.

But psychologists didn't only begin studying what was right with human behavior. Embracing the philosophy of positive psychology, Dr. Donald Clifton and other researchers at the Gallup Organization began studying not only individuals who were psychologically healthy but those who were able to accomplish near perfect performance in a range of work-related activities. After conducting over two million interviews with these individuals, certain patterns of behavior became evident, and researchers were able to identify thirty-four such patterns, or talents (Buckingham and Clifton 2001,11). These include, for example, "Activator," which refers to the ability to "make things happen by turning thoughts into action"; "Consistency," which is being "keenly aware of the need to treat people the same"; and "Relator," which refers to people who "enjoy close relationships with others." (A complete list of these talents is included in the appendix.) If, the researchers reasoned, it was possible for people to intentionally develop talents like these into strengths, not only at work but outside of it as well, it could provide them with a means of achieving their greatest potential. This, essentially, was the beginning of the Strengths Movement.

The Gallup Organization researchers also recognized, however, that these talents do not function in isolation. Through the use of the Strengths Finder assessment, a tool designed to help people discover their specific talents, they found that every individual possesses dominant talents which when used together can help achieve a goal. Imagine, for example, a man who possesses the talents of "Competition" and "Developer," and who coaches children's soccer in his spare time. "Competition" refers to people who "measure their progress against the performance of others" and "strive to win first place and revel in contests." "Developer" describes the individual who is able to "recognize and cultivate the potential in others." Not surprisingly, the coach's "Competition" talent helps the team set the goal of coming in first, and develop the winning mentality that it needs to do so. And his "Developer" talent helps him cultivate the potential in each one of the kids on the team and helps them grow and develop. It is the combination of these two talents make him be a better, more effective coach.

DEVELOPING STRENGTHS

Recognizing our talents is the first step on the path to excellence, but it's only the beginning. The next step is to develop those talents into strengths. A strength in this context can be defined as the ability to perform near perfect performance in any given activity, not just by accomplishing specific goals but, rather, by achieving a consistent level of excellence (Clifton, Anderson and Schreiner 2006, 4). Think about those who are the very best in their fields or activities. Although they often appear to attain their goals effortlessly, the fact is that every one of them has spent years of hard work developing their talents until they are able to accomplish those great things.

Exactly how do we develop our talents into strengths? We do it first by gaining knowledge and by applying skill to that knowledge. Knowledge can be both factual and experimental. Factual knowledge provides the foundation, and experimental knowledge provides the experience. Skill enables us to bring together both kinds of knowledge and begin to take the necessary steps to accomplish a particular task or activity (Clifton, Anderson and Schreiner 2006, 4). In fact, accomplishing almost any task requires the combination of talent, knowledge, and skill. For example, the soccer coach with the talents of "Competition" and "Developer" may build knowledge by reading about how coaches create a winning mind set and develop skills in players (factual knowledge), try various techniques (experimental knowledge), and then combine what he's learned with the techniques that work best with his players (skill). In doing so his "Competition" and "Developer" talents become strengths, and he becomes a better coach.

The first step in gaining knowledge is developing a good understanding of our talents and how they have surfaced in our lives. And the best way to do that is to reflect on our past experiences. The next chapter, "Exploring Our Talents," provides a means of doing that through the examination of four key concepts: the combination of our talents, how we use our talents in the balcony and basement, how our talents affect—and are affected—by our relationships, and how our talents enable us to survive the difficult times in our lives.

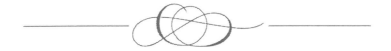

What makes a river so restful to people
is that it doesn't have any doubt-
it is sure to get where it is going,
and it doesn't want to go anywhere else.

-HAL BOYLE

CHAPTER TWO

Exploring Our Talents

$\mathcal{W}$e all possess talents, that is, patterns of thoughts, feelings or behaviors that we make use of in a broad range of circumstances (Clifton, Anderson and Schreiner 2006, 2). Unfortunately, few of us realize that these patterns *are* talents, or that these talents can be combined to enable us to grow and develop to our greatest potential. So how do we recognize these talents, and how do we learn to make use of them? In this instance, the past is the key to the future. By examining four aspects of our personal history we can see not only how we used our talents in the past but, even more important, how we can use them going forward. The four aspects to review are:

- How our talents joined together to create a powerful combination
- How we have used our talents in the balcony and basement
- How our talents have affected and been affected by our relationships
- How our talents have enabled us to survive the difficult times in our lives

By addressing these aspects of our past we will be able to build the foundation necessary to become the best versions of ourselves, and use our talents to get us where we want to go.

THE COMBINATION OF OUR TALENTS

Not only do we all possess a range of talents, but each of those talents has the potential to be enhanced by interaction with our other talents. As we face the different kinds of challenges we all must deal with over the course of our lives, we learn to combine our talents so that we can accomplish a variety of tasks, from making our relationships work to achieving success in our careers. How do we do this? Think again about the analogy of the river. The river consists of tributaries, bends, rocks, and falls that combine to guide it in its journey to the sea. Our talents are like those tributaries, bends, and rocks in that they combine to take us in the direction we need to go. And it's in this combination of talents is where our true potential lies.

Jeremiah's story provides a vivid illustration of how our talents join together and how those combinations impact on our lives. Living in a neighborhood where "something was always going on," and surrounded by gang influence and drug activity, Jeremiah grew up in a world in which young people focused primarily on survival. With little or no hope for college, few of those around him saw any reason to take high school seriously. As a result, Jeremiah would often tell his mother he was going to school when he was actually planning to spend the day hanging out with his friends, where he would find the support he needed to deal with his environment. And yet, his life eventually took a very different direction. After dropping out of high school, Jeremiah was content with a series of dead-end jobs until, one day, he passed a college campus on his way to work. Watching the students walking across campus with their books and backpacks, it seemed to him that they all had a purpose, something that was lacking in his own life. Visualizing a different future for himself, he began taking the necessary steps to enroll in college.

16

How did Jeremiah end up on such a different path? The answer lies in his talents and how those talents combined to lead his life in a positive direction. Although his talent of "Includer" led him into relationships with peers caught up in a world of gangs and drugs, his talent of "Responsibility" fueled his work ethic, and his talent of "Futuristic" enabled him to glimpse what his future would be like if he went to college. Together, these three talents laid the foundation necessary for him to pursue a better life. In fact, Jeremiah's story is a good example of how the combination of talents can provide a balancing act, with one talent ("Includer") potentially leading to trouble and others ("Responsibility" and "Futuristic") providing the ability to stay on track.

This should make it clear, then, that talents cannot and do not exist in isolation. The true power of our talents lies in their interaction and how that interaction strengthens each individual talent. Determining how our talents interact is a key component to building a strength-based life. Becoming the best versions of ourselves requires the use of all of our talents merged together to create the power of the combination. Although the use of one talent may bring a level of success, the use of our combination of talents offers the opportunity to achieve a level of excellence that will elude us if we choose to only use our talents in isolation.

THE BALCONY AND BASEMENT USE OF TALENT

Although our talents offer us a path to reach our greatest potential, the same talents must be used in positive, healthy situations. Used, for example, to maintain unhealthy relationships, talents will not only fail to enhance our lives but can even facilitate harmful—and even dangerous—situations. The irony is that whenever we are using our talents, things feel natural, as though we're on the path we should be taking, even though it may actually be to our disadvantage. We can all reflect on those times where we went down the wrong road or became entangled in an unhealthy relationship. But why do we sometimes go in the wrong direction? Examining the difficult times in our lives through the lens of our talents can provide us with insight into when and how we use those talents in environments, relationships, and activities that are contrary to their intended purpose.

Sheri, a forty-one-year-old single mother of four, provides a powerful example of the contradictory nature of talents. As a teenager she had gotten involved with the wrong crowd and, even though she had dreamed of going to college, dropped out of school in the seventh grade. But when she was twenty, married, and with two children, she came to the conclusion that she had achieved nothing in her life, and decided to pursue her GED in order to get a high school diploma. Excited about obtaining a high school diploma, Sheri remembered her dream of graduating from college and enrolled in a certificate program at a local community college. Regardless of the weather, Sheri walked to class every day, refusing to miss even one day of the education that had once eluded her. After completing a certificate in business, she set a goal for herself of working in an office.

However, Sheri's husband wanted her to remain at home, and in hopes of maintaining peace between them, she let go of her dreams. But her efforts were fruitless, and after years of struggling in an abusive relationship, and the birth of two more children, she left her husband. Going back to work, she held a number of low-paying dead-end jobs, working with individuals whom she describes as mean. Her difficulties eventually led her back to her dream of getting a college education, and finally she enrolled in a local university.

Sheri's story provides a dramatic example of the basement nature of our talents. Caught in an abusive relationship, she tried to use her talent of "Harmony"—seeking areas of agreement—in a desperate effort to avoid conflict in her marriage. Even after she left her husband, she continued to seek situations, such as work environments where there was considerable conflict and friction, in which she could use her talent. It was only when Sheri enrolled in college that she began to use several of her other talents, including "Consistency," indicated by her commitment to attend classes, "Learner," as shown by her excitement and dedication to school, and "Achiever," demonstrated by obtaining her GED and enrolling in a local community college.

Sheri also provides a good example of the difference between what are called balcony and basement qualities. Both balcony and basement qualities can produce life-changing effects, although dramatically different ones. Basement qualities—in Sheri's case "Harmony"—not only don't enhance personal development, they are actually detrimental and, in some situations, can even be life threatening. Balcony qualities, on the other hand, contribute to an individual's overall well-being and development. They make it possible for people to have healthy and productive relationships, work at jobs that enable them to make the best use of their talents, and use those talents in ways that enhance the community. In Sheri's case, it was life as a college student that provided her with the means to exercise her balcony qualities of "Consistency," "Learner," and "Achiever."

As noted above, though, even using basement qualities may feel comfortable, because the individual is still using his or her innate abilities. We tend to be drawn to individuals who bring out our talents even if, as in Sheri's case, her talent of "Harmony" led her into a dysfunctional relationship. Other examples might include people exercising a talent to move a career forward by using unethical methods or by hurting others within the organization, or people in community organizations using their talents not for the greater good but for individual gain or profit. So care must be used with our talents. Used in healthy environments, positive relationships and constructive activities, they can provide a foundation for becoming our personal best. But used in detrimental environments, relationships and activities, they can become destructive, hurting not only ourselves but others along the way. Our talents represent our potential, but we have to determine how that potential will be utilized.

TALENTS AND RELATIONSHIPS

As with many other aspects of our lives, our relationships can affect and be affected by the use of our talents, both positively and negatively. If you think about it, it's likely that you will be able to remember people in your life who brought out the best—and possibly the worst—in you. Sometimes relationships serve as an impetus for the positive development of our talents, and provide just the motivation or encouragement we need to move towards a strengths-based life. However, relationships can also move us in the opposite direction, that is, be a catalyst to use our talents to our detriment. The end result may differ, but both represent examples of our talents impacting on, and being impacted by, the relationships in our lives.

The relationship between sixteen-year-old Corina and her high school principal offers a vivid illustration of how relationships can trigger the use of our talents. Believing that her teachers didn't care about her, and that they saw her as just one of the crowd, Corina developed a lack of interest in school. Not surprisingly, all of this impacted on her academic performance, and during her sophomore year she completed only four of the fifty required credits. Forced to attend night school to catch up, she decided to transfer to a different high school in the community for a fresh start.

In her new school Corina joined various student clubs and organizations, including the student newspaper, honor societies, and the League of United Latin American Citizens. She also participated in the Educational Talent Search Program, which is designed to increase high school graduation and college enrollment rates of first-generation, low-income students. Through this program, Corina began taking the necessary steps towards enrollment in college after graduation. Before long, though, she fell back into her old habits, connecting with a group of students with little interest in school, and began ditching classes. The school's principal brought her into his office, told her that he did not see her graduating, and suggested she "stop wasting their time and just drop out." He handed her a form to drop out of school, but Corina refused to sign it.

Instead of discouraging Corina from completing high school, the interaction with the principal provided her with a new motivation to complete high school. She stopped ditching classes, focused on school, and began seeking out the principal in the school's crowded hallways, making a point of speaking to him. Late in her senior year, Corina got pregnant, but she continued attending school and kept her pregnancy a secret so the principal would not believe that she had given up on school. She did graduate, and when she walked across the stage to receive her diploma from the principal, she looked him squarely in the eye and asked if he remembered her. He told her that he did, and that he was very proud of her.

Corina's story is a good example of how a relationship can impact on a talent. Even before Corina changed schools she had demonstrated several of her talents, including "Learner"—the desire to learn and improve—through her love of books when she was a young child. But it was only after she changed schools, and fell back into her old habits, that the principal's challenge to her commitment to education reignited her other talents. It was then that she demonstrated "Responsibility" and "Belief"—having unchanging core values—by re-committing herself to school, and "Relator"—enjoying close relationships—as she sought out the principal on a regular basis. Although this strategy could have easily created a different response in another student, for Corina the interaction served as a wake-up call about the importance of graduating from high school.

Because relationships are critical to our personal growth and development, they play an extraordinarily important role in each of our lives. Although there have been several theorists in the field of human development who believe that relationships guide us through the normal developmental stages we face in our lives, one of the most respected of these is Erik Erickson, who developed the Psychosocial Crisis Cycle Model (Erikson 1959). According to this model, beginning as infants and continuing through our senior years, we all go through eight stages in which we face specific types of challenges and learn specific types of lessons:

Stage One - Hope: Trust vs. Mistrust

Stage Two - Will: Autonomy vs. Shame and Doubt

Stage Three - Purpose: Initiative vs. Guilt

Stage Four - Competence: Industry vs. Inferiority

Stage Five - Fidelity: Identity vs. Role Confusion
Stage Six - Love: Intimacy vs. Isolation
Stage Seven - Care: Generativity vs. Stagnation
Stage Eight - Wisdom: Integrity vs. Despair

Relationships are not, however, only important to our overall development. They are also very important in the development of our talents during the various stages of our lives. The first three stages Erickson identified occur at a very early age, when our talents are first evident. Naturally drawn to experiences and information that tap into their talents, children have an innate understanding of what their talents are, but they need parents to help provide the structure necessary for their development. In the first stage, which concerns "Hope," we must develop trust versus mistrust, and the relationship with the mother is central to doing so. In the second, which Erickson labeled "Will," autonomy versus shame and doubt represent the primary challenge, and our important relationships expand to include both parents. The third stage is "Purpose," during which we have to deal with initiative versus guilt, and represents the point in our lives when critical relationships extend to the entire family. During this stage we begin to take initiative in play activities, role playing what it is like to be an adult.

In the next two stages relationships outside the family become more important. In Stage Four, which Erickson labeled "Competence," we deal with the challenge of industry versus inferiority. At this stage we develop confidence in our ability to learn, and relationships with teachers, friends, classmates, and others in the neighborhood provide the support, encouragement, and structure necessary to remain on a strengths path. In the fifth stage, "Fidelity," which usually occurs during adolescence, we struggle with the developmental task of identity, with the primary relationship shifting to our peers. This can be a challenging period, since peer pressure may not be particularly focused on the development of our talents into strengths. It can also be a period during which we invest our talents in environments, relationships and activities that are unhealthy and sometimes even destructive.

The three remaining stages occur during adulthood, with the focus shifting from family, to career, to community. During Stage Six, "Love," the primary challenge is between intimacy and isolation, and our intimate relationships can bring out our best or worst. Such relationships can provide the positive experiences and knowledge necessary to develop and enhance our talents, but they can also work to our detriment, providing little encouragement to the development of talents or encouraging us to invest our talents in environments and activities that are counter to our growth and development. In Stage Seven, which Erickson called "Care," the relationships of greatest importance are those with our supervisors and colleagues at work, who can provide a supportive environment and offer experiences and knowledge critical to the development of talents. On the other hand, if they don't provide this support and guidance, the individual can be left feeling frustrated. The eighth and final stage is "Wisdom," the time during which we must work to develop integrity rather than despair. This is when we reflect on our lives, and feel either a sense of fulfillment because of our accomplishments or a sense of frustration due to our failures. In this stage it is the relationships we develop in schools, churches, recreation programs, and various community organizations that can offer additional opportunities for the development of our talents and provide us with an outlet for our talents through service to the community.

As Erickson's model shows, relationships are not only a critical component of our overall growth and development, but of the growth of our talents into strengths. Just as with other endeavors in our lives, we need individuals around us, serving a variety of roles, to help us change and grow. For some, this may mean relationships full of love and support, encouraging us to learn new ideas and try new experiences. For others, these relationships may provide challenges, a subtle or blatant call for change. Either way, individuals who see our talents, and find ways to facilitate the cultivation of those talents, help us to transform those talents into strengths.

OVERCOMING LIFE'S DIFFICULTIES

Although we are often not aware of it at the time, our talents can also play a pivotal role in helping us overcome life's difficulties. If you think about all the times that you have experienced difficulty in your life, you will probably see that you approached the difficulties in the same manner, and used similar behaviors to help you get through them. You probably also experienced the same flood of emotions, and went through the same thought processes each time in your efforts to get past the pain. Those behaviors, feelings, and thoughts are actually your talents guiding you through life's challenges.

Dan's story provides a powerful example of how our talents can help us in difficult times. At the relatively young age of thirty-five, this married father of three was diagnosed with colon cancer, and he knew that his life would change forever. Not only would he have to find a way to beat the disease, but, because he would no longer be able to do the kind of physically intensive work that he did, he would have to find a new career path. Fortunately, Dan had already developed several talents that would guide him during this difficult period in his life. During middle and high school he had participated in sports, in the process developing the talent of "Competition," which enabled him to believe that he could be successful in his battle against cancer. He had also developed two other very useful talents. He developed the first, "Deliberative"—the ability to be very careful in making decisions, and the second, "Maximizer"—the ability to focus on strengths, by the approach he took in his career choices. Combining these talents with his "Competition" talent, he was able to not only battle his cancer but to find a new direction for his life, enrolling in a community college so that he could re-enter the workforce with different career goals and focus.

The first four semesters of college were very difficult for Dan. He underwent two major surgeries for the cancer, which rid him of the disease, but he still suffered from complications, and was ill at the end of every semester. Twice he ended up in the hospital, once during finals week. Even so, he persisted, graduating with an associate degree and with plans to transfer to a four-year institution to pursue a BA in Communications. He is currently still an undergraduate, but has long-range plans to go on to graduate school. Dan's story is a good example of how the talents of "Competition," "Deliberative," and "Maximizer" combined to provide him with the strength he needed to not only win over a potentially life-ending illness, but to turn this crisis into a new direction for his life.

In this chapter we've explored how our talents interact, how we sometimes use those talents in the balcony and basement, how our talents impact—and are impacted by—our relationships, and how our talents help enable us to get through difficult periods in our lives. As noted in the previous chapter, exploring these four areas provides us with a means of gaining both factual and experimental knowledge of ourselves and how we've used our talents, which is the first step in developing our talents into strengths. The next step is to use our skills to bring together both types of knowledge and apply them to accomplishing a particular task or activity. In the following chapters you will find the stories of nine individuals who took that next step. These stories will not only provide vivid illustrations of how we use our talents in each of the four areas, but will also enable you to gain the skills necessary to examine the important roles your talents have played, and can play, in your life.

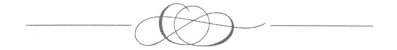

RIVERS are roads that move and carry us
WHITHER WE WISH TO GO

-BLAISE PASCAL

CHAPTER THREE

Mike

POSITIVITY – ADAPTABILITY – WOO – EMPATHY

"The perfect storm" may sound like an unusual description for a series of difficult, life-altering events, but that's how Mike, age fifty, describes a period during which he experienced a tremendous amount of loss, only to discover a new direction for his life. As Mike tells the story:

> My second wife and I married in 1991. We each brought children with us. She had one child and I brought four with me. Then we had two children of our own. She was diagnosed with cancer in 2001. Prior to her being diagnosed, we'd bought a house. We were buying for prestige rather than what we could afford. And when she was diagnosed, she lost her job. We had no equity in the house, and we had no way to keep up with the payments, so we lost it. We ended up in a low-income house donated to us by the church. And that was kind of a hard shock to take. And then she died, on September 1, 2004, and left me with two young girls to raise in that little house. I didn't know

27

what I was going to do, but I had a pretty good job and the future looked fairly bright. At that time it was just, "Tough it out, we're going to make it." But a year later, I was laid off. That was a big moment.

After experiencing this series of events, in an effort to alleviate depression and stress, Mike began training for the triathlon. Not long after, he was out riding his bicycle one day and took a wrong turn, ending up on a community college campus. Spotting the building on campus that housed the welding program, he went into the building, thinking that he might be able to build a new bike. Inside he met an instructor with whom he felt an immediate bond, which was very unlike the reaction he usually had when meeting teachers. Immediately seeing Mike's potential, the instructor encouraged him to apply for admission to the college and declare welding as his major. Taking no time to think through the implications, Mike went directly to the Admissions Office and started the application process. College would be the opportunity for a better future.

A LIFE'S JOURNEY

Mike claims he had an "Opie Taylor" childhood. Born in 1957, he grew up in a small town in Texas near the Oklahoma border—the only boy among seven children. His father had dropped out of high school in 1942 to fight in World War II, and after the war worked as a truck driver. His mother finished high school but she never went to college, and she worked as a cashier at the local grocery store. The family lived modestly, and, according to Mike, his parents "worked like dogs."

My parents are from the Greatest Generation. They're from that generation that's loyal to the country, and they took some hard, hard knocks. My parents were born to parents who weren't that far removed from the Civil War, so they had an entirely different mind set. They were born in the 'Twenties, and they could have starved. That was a reality to them. Starvation was a reality. It's not for us. None of us have ever experienced anything close to hunger. There's really no excuse for any of us from my generation to experience hunger. And to them, an education was the stuff that books are written about. If you have an education then you have really arrived. You really have obtained something.

In 1962, when he was five, Mike's parents bought what he describes as a "junky old farmhouse." It was a two-storey frame house that was not only in need of painting but also cold and drafty. Only the living room had a heater, and what heat there was in the kitchen came from the stove. Even so, when asked if his family was low income, Mike says "Boy, that's a tough one." Although money was tight, Mike and his sisters were always able to participate in Boy Scouts, Girl Scouts, Little League, or community programs and events. While his parents "worked their hands to the bones," Mike recalls that they always got by:

We always managed to dress in style as kids. And I grew up with sisters so it was real important to them. And we always had wonderful Christmases. I can remember many of them. I remember some of the gifts from all of them. And we always had birthdays, we always had presents for our birthdays.

Family vacations consisted of Mike's father piling all the kids into the car to go to California to visit family, then driving up to Seattle to see their grandfather before heading back home.

Every summer. That was etched in stone. And I vaguely remember the benchmark was $200. We had to have that $200 to make the trip. I remember where the can was where they would hide the money. Mom would save half dollars and silver dollars, and, of course, I would get in there and steal some of it. That's the way she saved money.

THE DUMB WHITE KID

Mike remembers the names of every one of his teachers from first grade on, including the principal and music teacher, noting that "all these people stand out in my mind." Although he particularly remembers a few teachers who believed he had potential as a student, elementary school was overall a difficult experience:

> First and foremost, I sucked at going to school. I've always considered myself academically stupid, and I struggled through school from day one. But I excelled in having friends, and I excelled at recess. I did good with that. I was also good at storytelling and at writing. When I read a story I wrote I would have the class in the palm of my hand.

Mike's early school experience is a good example of the first glimpses of talent. Using his talents of " WOO"—winning others over—and " Positivity"—having enthusiasm that is contagious, Mike discovered his ability to connect and communicate with others. Academics may have been a struggle, but his ability to form relationships with others was something he did well.

The integration of his elementary school provided Mike with an opportunity to demonstrate another one of his talents— "Empathy," the ability to sense the feelings of others. Mike recalls the first day that African American students were admitted, and the teacher selecting the story "Little Black Sambo" to read to the class. When the teacher came to the racial slurs in the story all the children turned to look at the expressions on the faces of the three African American students. But Mike felt what he describes as a "kinship" with these students, feeling he was also labeled, although in his case it was as one of the stupid kids. Speaking of the racial divide at the time, he remembers:

> We couldn't care about that stuff. We were kids. And the boys could play ball, they could catch. The little girl was sharp as a whip, but did she ever get called on in class? Never. I never saw

their papers but I'm assuming that they got minimal remarks. And, so, yeah, a lot of mistakes in school. That's the kind of mistakes I saw.

By the time Mike got to third grade his difficulty with academics had grown even worse. Referring to himself as "the dumb white kid," Mike remembers his teacher telling him that he needed to repeat the third grade.

She called me up to the desk and asked me if I'd ever been— How did she say it?—"retained." I told her I hadn't, and she said, "Okay, sit down." And then she called up a girl and another boy. And I kind of figured it out. It's like, okay, it's us three. We're the ones that really don't get the grades. And so I put it together in my head. I didn't know what retained meant, but after I saw who was called up to the desk, it was, "Okay, I get it. So I'm going to flunk."

Even though Mike had already exhibited several of his talents by the time he was in third grade, his teachers completely failed to recognize them. So instead of finding ways to use his talents to improve his academic performance, they gave him the "dumb white kid" label, and provided him with none of the encouragement that might have made him feel he could be a good student. Not surprisingly, Mike's self-image suffered, and that negative self-perception carried on into high school.

JUST GET HIM A JOB WITH A SHOVEL

The problems Mike encountered in elementary school also continued into high school. He spent two years in the ninth grade due to attendance issues, primarily because he spent most of his day hanging out at the "smoking dock" rather than going to class.

It was the Seventies. We were smoking dope and drinking lots of beer. I was an ornery kid. Just an ornery kid in a small town. We were mischievous, but we didn't steal things, we didn't vandalize things other than toilet papering houses or stealing trash cans. We did steal this one guy's car a few times for about a month. We'd skip school and drive the car up to Oklahoma, go to the falls and go swimming, and then bring it back. And he never caught on.

Although he received no encouragement from his teachers in high school, Mike believed he was doing better the year he repeated the ninth grade. He credits his girlfriend, whom he later married, with helping him to focus more on academics. He particularly remembers a success he experienced in speech class:

I remember that speech class, and giving my first speech, and how excited my teacher was about it. I did it the way she told us to do it, and I nailed it. I was making a great speech, and the teacher was really fired up about it. And I was like, Wow! Then a teacher from the Building Trades Department came and pulled me out of the class, and told me I'd be better off there. I wasn't getting the marks, you know, and I was the kind of guy that they said "Let's get him a job with a shovel." And I was, like, "Okay, I'll go over here and I'll do whatever you say. I'm just a dumb white kid." But they goofed up, they made a mistake. I'm not one to point fingers, but I think they made a mistake.

In high school Mike continued to exhibit the talents of "WOO," "Positivity," and "Empathy," together creating a combination that gave him the ability to connect with people. But he also exhibited the talent of "Adaptability"—the ability to go with the flow, as demonstrated by his reaction to being removed from the speech class. Although this was one of the few times Mike did well, he was, as he put it, "okay" with the decision to move him out of the class. Unfortunately, Mike's poor relationships with teachers continued to impact his ability to use and develop his talents.

In 1975, Mike's girlfriend got pregnant, so he dropped out of school, got married, and began working as a bricklayer's helper. His job consisted of laying bricks, mixing mortar, and setting up scaffolding. On weekends, Mike would pick pecans for beer money, which was "brutal work on hands and knees." A series of jobs followed, including working with a moving company, then a shoe company, driving trucks, working for a seismograph company, and as a welder for a boilermaker company. In regard to his career up to this point, Mike says:

> Mostly as I was getting older, it was about learning a trade. I just wanted to learn a trade. I had been working with bricklayers quite a bit and it was strictly a young man's job. At the time it wasn't a bad living. It wasn't a bad endeavor to learn a trade. And I had always been fascinating with welding.

Over time, Mike and his wife had four children, but they subsequently divorced, and he remarried in 1991. He and his second wife had two children of their own, but then, in 2001, she contracted cancer, and died three years later. At the time, despite all his difficulties, Mike felt that he and the children would be all right. And then, a year after that, he lost his job as a welder with a local building contractor. It was at that point that he realized what he'd been experiencing was a "perfect storm." These events could easily have devastated Mike and his family, but by combining his talents of "Positivity" and "Adapt-ability" Mike was able to find a way to cope with them, and to not only survive but to find a new, positive direction for his life.

AFTER THE STORM

Having weathered his "perfect storm," and enrolled in college, Mike found himself facing a mixed reaction from his family. While his parents were primarily concerned about how he would support his children, his two daughters were very excited for their father. As Mike explains:

> Dad was a bit suspicious of the whole thing. Mom was like, "Well okay, but how are you going to make a living?" And you know that was their biggest concern—how we were going to take care of the kids while I was going to school. And I honestly didn't know. I still had two daughters at home, one in high

school, and one in the second grade. The high school daughter, of course, was going through everything that a high school girl goes through at that time. She had just lost her mother, so she was struggling, but she thought it was pretty cool that her dad was going to college, even though it was a community college. And the youngest, she ate it up. She loved it.

Having struggled with school since he was a child, and considering himself "academically stupid," Mike found his first days on campus to be "terrifying." But as he got accustomed to it, things got easier for him. As he explains:

At least in the welding department, I came into the classroom with an edge. I knew how to weld and I knew how to weld well. Still, I went into that classroom to learn the technical side of welding. I could do "monkey see, monkey do" welding. I've done that most of my life. Now it was time to learn why the monkey was doing it.

As it's turned out, Mike has been very successful in college, with a cumulative grade point average of 3.4. A highlight of his academic career was being inducted into Phi Theta Kappa, the national honor society. He sent the induction letter he received to his mother, who cried while reading it. But Mike also entered college determined to get involved in everything it had to offer. During his second year, he was elected student body president, which he considers to be his biggest success in college. In this role, Mike serves as the voice of students on the Board of Trustees, and he is considered to be very effective at it. In addition, when the state legislature attempted a dramatic reduction in the institution's budget, he led a successful protest that led to the reinstatement of the funding. His success in student government particularly surprises him:

You know, who would have thought? Who would have thought? That's huge, that's huge stuff. And I'm good at it. I am. I find I'm a fairly good problem solver, and a pretty good people manager. I'm managing my office, and my executive board, as well as could be expected. It's awesome. Something comes up almost daily—either a student or something on the executive board that I have to deal with. And I'm finding out that when I go in front of the Board of Trustees every month I can do it, and I can do it well.

The academic and social connections Mike has established on campus have also provided him with the sense of belonging that was missing in his previous educational experiences. As he explains:

It's given me a sense of ownership. I'm invested in this college. I see cups and stuff on campus and I'll bend over and pick them up. This is my campus. This is my college. I'm a member of the English Honor Society. We're the ones who stand up and read those hokey poems. Some of them are good, some are dumb, but we have a blast doing it.

So after thirty years, Mike has discovered a learning environment that provides him with the opportunity to use his talents, and as a result has become a successful student. Using his talents of "Positivity," "WOO," "Empathy," and "Adaptability," he has also found a perfect fit for his combination as the student body president. Finally, although he once thought he'd be a "labor guy" for the rest of his life, Mike now sees himself as a middle school English teacher and cross country coach. But he believes that college has changed him in other ways as well:

My hands are softer. I don't bleed as often. Also, my thinking processes are different. I believe I'm more open minded now, and I can look at things in a lot of different ways than I did before. I analyze situations differently, too. And my idea of who and what I am has changed. When the time comes, I will be able to write a report, and write it well. When the time comes, I will be able to stand in front a classroom and teach them, and teach them well. If you had asked me a year or two ago to write down what I expected from college, I would have sold myself short. But it's been everything and more. The main thing is, now I know I can learn. I know I can learn."

THE ROLE OF TALENT

Mike's talents of "Positivity," "Adaptability," "WOO", and "Empathy" are evident in his life's journey. Beginning in elementary school, he demonstrated his ability to connect with others by using "Positivity," "WOO," and "Empathy." Unfortunately, none of his teachers—from elementary school through high school—was able to recognize any of his specific talents. The most distressing example occurred in a high school speech class, when he began to develop some confidence only to be moved out of the class to a building trades course. His experiences in school did, however, enable him to learn to use the talents of "Positivity" and "Adaptability" to get through difficult times. This combination of talents became critical later in his life when he had to deal with a series of difficult events he described as "the perfect storm." Using his talents, Mike was able to navigate through a series of life-changing events, leading to his enrollment in a community college. And it was there that Mike finally discovered a learning environment that supported the use of all his talents, enabled him to become a successful student, and led him to the realization that, as he put it, "I know I can learn."

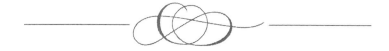

Never give up; for even rivers
someday wash dams.

– ARTHUR GOLDEN

CHAPTER FOUR

Adriana

EMPATHY-POSITIVITY-WOO-
DEVELOPER-INCLUDER

Sitting in the county jail, Adriana, age thirty-four, knew the
time had come to change her life. A young mom with the
goal of becoming a registered nurse, she had worked at a variety
of jobs, most recently at a local communications company. It was
while working there that she had spiraled into the world of drugs,
where "all the goals and stuff just blew out the window." Addicted
to methamphetamine, Adriana was arrested for check fraud, a
crime she committed while trying to buy drugs. She was sentenced
to three months in jail. As she explains:

> I had a lot of problems with the law and with drugs. I was in
> jail and I was being moved to a community corrections facility,
> and I'm thinking, "I don't want to do this. I want to change my
> life. I want it to go in a positive direction, and I can't do any-
> thing better than finally going to college." While I was in jail,
> a woman from the Educational Opportunity Center came to
> talk to us, and she helped me do my application for admission

to college and all my financial aid stuff. And that's really how it got going.

Excited about the chance to transform her own life by going to college, Adriana became convinced that education could be a path for others as well. If she could change her life, she thought, others could too. Seeing the potential of her fellow inmates, she convinced several women who were completing jail sentences to submit college applications and apply for financial aid. This effort was actually a demonstration of several of Adriana's talents, including "Developer"—cultivating the potential in others, and "WOO"—winning others over. It also exhibited her talents of "Includer"—accepting and including of others, and "Positivity"—having enthusiasm that's contagious.

A LIFE'S JOURNEY

Adriana, who identifies herself as Hispanic, grew up in a family with one older sister and two brothers. Her father, who was from Mexico, left school after the fourth grade, and her mother, who had been born in the United States, dropped out in the ninth grade. Notwithstanding their own experience—or perhaps because of it—her parents felt very strongly about the benefits of education. As she explains:

Both of my parents think it is extremely important. Neither one of them had the opportunity to go to college. Neither one of them, and they wanted to. They had dreams and goals just like everyone else does. My mom had to drop out because her family was so poor. She had to go work in the fields, onion fields or whatever. My dad was left homeless in Mexico, left homeless for about four years, he and his brother. He wanted to go to school to become an airplane mechanic, or something in aviation. My mom really had low self-esteem because she couldn't help us with our homework. So it was definitely important in our household.

40

When Adriana was six-years-old, her parents got divorced, and the children had to choose to live with either their mother or their father. Adriana describes the family after the divorce:

My mom was pretty poor and she lived in housing on the north side of town, apartments. My dad was always the bread winner of the family, and when they divorced he kept the house. He always made good money. At first, when they got divorced, my brothers stayed with my dad and I stayed with my mom, but we all kind of ended up with my mom. I remember there were cockroaches in the apartment. But as far as clothes, money, allowance, food, my dad would provide that. We grew up kind of feeling like my dad would provide the financial part of our growing up. My mom was all about love and all that.

When Adriana's mother was thirty-five she was diagnosed with rheumatoid arthritis and found it difficult to work. Receiving only $400 to $500 dollars a month in social security, she couldn't make ends meet. So her mother began delivering newspapers, getting up between two and three in the morning to deliver the papers, and then, later in the day, working in the newspaper office.

A LIFE SPIRALING OUT OF CONTROL

Adriana recalls always doing well in school, but junior high school marked the beginning of a change. In part because of her talent as an "Includer," she fell in with a group of other teenagers who smoked marijuana, an example of how people sometimes invest their talents to their detriment, in this case negative relationships. The pattern continued into high school, where Adriana would leave school with her friends to get drunk, smoke marijuana, and, eventually, experiment with methamphetamine. As she says:

So I was going to high school. I was doing really good at the beginning. When I got to high school, it was easy to leave campus. A lot of us would go and get drunk and smoke weed. And that's when I first got into meth. And I started to get sexually active and got pregnant.

Adriana was fifteen when she got pregnant. Believing she would not fit in when others learned of her pregnancy, she left school before she started to show. As a result, though, she fell so far behind academically that she was forced to drop out of school altogether. Refusing to quit, Adriana continued her education through a local alternative school that had a daycare center where she could leave her daughter. She passed her GED, and had plans to become a registered nurse. Instead, she had two more children, and worked in several different companies, including a local meat packing company and a communications firm. In both companies she was moved from one shift to another, which made it difficult to establish any kind of consistent routine. It was while working the graveyard shift in the communications company that her life spiraled deeper into the world of drugs, leading eventually to her arrest and imprisonment.

A LIFE TRANSFORMED

Having completed all the necessary paperwork for admission to community college while serving time in county jail, Adriana began to contemplate a different future. And when she learned she'd been admitted to the college, she was thrilled. As she explains, "I was very proud. Very proud. I was thinking, 'Wow, just five or six months ago there was no way to go back, and now I may be going to school.'" Her reaction represents a good example of her talent of "Positivity." That is, instead of focusing on her past, she chose to focus on the progress she had made in turning her life in a new direction.

Adriana started her first semester at community college at the same time that she began serving her sentence at a nearby half way house. Like all first-time college students, she was nervous, but the nervousness she experienced went beyond the norm. As she puts it:

I was definitely nervous. I was both excited and nervous at the same time. I was thinking about my age. You know, I was going to be in school with all these young kids. I was also really nervous about my intellectual ability because of all the drugs. School learning had never been a problem for my brothers and me, but with all the drugs I had done I really thought I would have problems remembering things.

While living in the halfway house and attending school, Adriana also exhibited both the balcony and basement aspects of her talent of "Includer." Adriana found it difficult to be accepted by others, called "whitewashed" by other Latinos when she tried to study in the dining room. On the other hand, finding a positive environment for her talent, Adriana built a solid network of support on campus and began to feel she belonged in the community college environment.

It was really hard for someone in my situation—in community corrections, at my age, and just being off drugs for, what, six or seven months. It was nerve-racking coming here. But you get here, and you find that you blend in. There's a lot of people your age, and when you do your introductions in the classroom you start to learn that there's a lot of people that have been in the same situation as you—even kids who came from the same kind of background as you did, and kids who are young moms. Just like me, they wanted to do this, they want to become successful.

In addition to exhibiting the talents of "Positivity," "Includer," and "Developer," at this point Adriana also began to exhibit "Empathy," that is, "sensing the feelings of other people by imaging themselves in other's lives or situations." Having struggled with these talents in school and in the correctional facility, she could now see others trying to build a better life for themselves and their families, and feel the acceptance that had eluded her for so many years.

Determined to continue her pursuit of a college degree, Adriana got her mother to agree to take care of her children while she was completing her sentence at a local halfway house. Her brother was also very helpful since, having already graduated from college, he was able to provide answers to all the questions she had about school. In fact, it was her family's support, and her belief in God, that provided the additional assistance Adriana needed during this difficult period.

> Drawing on my faith really helped me get through it. Faith is a wonderful thing that you can't physically see, but you know it's there. Another thing was my mom and brother. My mom constantly reminded me that she was proud of me. She's still proud of me. She kept saying that it doesn't matter where you are now, but where you're going. She kept reassuring me that my kids were fine and I didn't have to worry about it. I should just focus on getting through, focus on the first semester of school.

Living apart from her three children while completing her sentence in the halfway house, Adriana not only felt the stress of being separated from them but also felt torn between her responsibilities as a mother and as a student. As she explains:

> I was having a lot of problems with my daughter, and one time [while living in the halfway house] I stopped by at home and I was thinking, "Why am I doing this? I should just stay home and worry about being a mom." That is, be there for them, because I hadn't been there for them. I was thinking, "It's too overwhelming. The parenting, the working, the school, the financial stress. I should quit all this and just go work."

Not only did Adriana feel torn between her responsibilities as a mother and a student, the men who fathered her children offered little support for her plans to pursue a college degree.

> My two exes—Victor and Dennis—didn't help at all. Especially Dennis. He would just flat out tell me that I'm stupid, I'm an idiot. Look where I'm at, I'm not going to succeed in college,

I don't have the smarts or the brains. Yeah, I should just give it up. And it was all because I wasn't there anymore, willing to please him. I was thinking, "Okay, I'm going to succeed in life. It's going to be about me, not about anybody else. I've got to work on me."

These experiences provided Adriana with an opportunity to use her talents of "Positivity" and "Developer" to help her stay in school. Even with the pressures of balancing motherhood and school, and getting no support from her children's fathers, Adriana used her "Positivity" to remain focused on completing her education. In addition, knowing that education would help her cultivate her own abilities, Adriana used her talent of "Developer" to focus on her own personal growth.

Unlike any of her earlier experiences, Adriana also found that the community college was an environment in which she could use her talent of "Includer" in a positive way. When she describes going out to lunch or coffee, or just hanging out at other student's homes, it becomes clear that the relationships she established with others on campus were dramatically different than the ones she'd had in junior high or high school. As she says:

Actually sitting down and having a conversation with someone for a long time just blows my mind. I'm serious. You can actually have fun without having a drink or doing a line or something. You're actually sitting there just having coffee or looking at your books, or studying or just talking. It's amazing. It's just so different.

College also gave Adriana "a total sense of accomplishment," and changed her entire outlook on life. "I have a completely different perspective on everything," she says. "Something as simple as a rock, it's not a rock anymore. Once you become educated about something, it's so much more to you."

Having completed her Associate Degree in Liberal Arts in Spring 2008, Adriana received a scholarship to the Stryker Institute for Leadership Development at the University of Northern Colorado, where she is pursuing a bachelor's degree in psychology. She's looking forward to obtaining a master's as well. Once she gets her master's, she is planning on a career working with troubled youths, particularly those who have been affected by violence and drugs. She believes the adolescent years are a critical time, and that many troubled youths are being raised in homes with parents who just don't care. Reflecting on her own past, and exhibiting her talent of "Empathy," Adriana says, "I want to help people change their lives. Nobody wants to be a mom at sixteen. Nobody wants to be in an abusive relationship. Nobody wants to be addicted to drugs and go to jail. It is the struggles that mold you into the person you are today."

THE ROLE OF TALENTS

Adriana's life journey demonstrates the use of her talents of "Includer," "Positivity," "Developer," "WOO," and "Empathy." Beginning in junior high school, her talent of "Includer" had critical implications for the relationships in her life. At first, using the basement of the talent, Adriana was drawn to the wrong crowd, which moved her life in the wrong direction. Later, however, in the new environment of a community college, she used the balcony of the talent to forge more positive relationships. Even before she started college, though, she made use of the talents of "Positivity," "Developer," and "WOO," not only by striving to make positive changes in her own life but also by encouraging others to do the same. And, finally, in anticipating what she will do when she attains a college degree, she uses the talent of "Empathy" to help others who have been in similarly difficult situations to overcome them and set themselves on a more positive path.

Ideas, like large rivers,
never have just one source.

-WILLIE LEY

CHAPTER FIVE

Jeremiah

RESTORATIVE-RESPONSIBILITY-
INCLUDER-FUTURISTIC-LEARNER

*H*igh school was just a place to "hang out" for Jeremiah, and after his mother caught him ditching school, she gave him an ultimatum: Go to school or get a job. Two weeks before graduation, Jeremiah dropped out. No one from the school called to find out what happened to him. He just left.

The first job he got was, as he put it, "busting his butt" pouring concrete, a job he stayed with for five years. The next was restoring automobile interiors, which he enjoyed. It was, in fact, during this period of his life that Jeremiah began demonstrating several of his talents. He demonstrated the talent of "Responsibility"—taking ownership for what one says he or she will do—by working steadily after his mother gave him the ultimatum to either go to school or get a job. He also exhibited the talent of "Restorative"—being able to figure out what is wrong and fix it—in restoring the interiors of cars. One day, though, after having an argument with his boss, he started looking for a new job. As he explains:

49

I started looking in the paper and I just realized that I had no skills. I couldn't get a decent job, you know. The best job I could get paid peanuts. It's pretty hard to get ahead if you can barely make enough to get by each week. Then I saw an ad in the classifieds for a free GED at a local college. So I called them and went in and talked to some lady and took the test. At that point, I was just going to get my GED, and I wasn't planning on going to college. But I got a really good score on the test, and she said, "Would you like to go to college? You'd be accepted with that score." And I said, "Well I can't afford going to college. I just want to get my GED so I can get a better job." She said, "Well, there's help for you if you really want to go," and I said, "If you're saying there's a way for me to go, I'll definitely go."

Jeremiah's effort to get his GED, and his decision to go on to college, reflect a combination of "Responsibility," "Restorative," and "Futuristic"—that is, being inspired by what the future can bring, in that he recognized that education was the best way for him to develop the skills he needed to get a better paying job. Thinking a small college would be the best place to start, Jeremiah connected with the Educational Opportunity Center to get help applying for admission and financial aid at a local community college. Several months later, he enrolled there.

A LIFE'S JOURNEY

Self-identified as Hispanic, Jeremiah grew up in a single-parent household with two older brothers. Money was tight, with his mother having to work two jobs to support the family. Sometimes, though, even that wasn't enough, and in order to save on rent the family moved often within the community. Jeremiah remembers attending two different elementary schools, two different middle schools, and one high school in the same area. He also recalls the family collecting welfare during periods when his mother was unemployed.

My mom did the best she could. She was never a bad mom. She was just in a bad situation. It was really hard for her to raise three children, especially because my brother, the middle one, was wild. He was always in trouble, the cops were always bringing him home, and he was always having to get bailed out of juvenile hall, or whatever it was. He went to prison when he was 18 and got out when he was 29. Then he went back for another year.

During his high school years, as Jeremiah describes it, his neighborhood was a place where "something was always going on." It was a poor, violent neighborhood where, because of the prevalence of gangs and drug activity, it was all one could do to survive. As a result, he grew up in an atmosphere of hopelessness.

I had my car broken into a lot of times. There were always fights, and a lot of drug activity. Looking back on it, it was just not a place where people considered that they could be successful. They just didn't think that way. There are other important things to take care of in your life before you can even consider an education, like surviving. You know what I mean. A lot of the people in the neighborhood just wanted to get a job and get paid, and didn't really think about further education.

Although Jeremiah considers himself to have been raised by a single parent, his mother was actually married for twenty-one years to a man he describes as an alcoholic. Jeremiah recalls the family having to deal with alcoholism everyday, explaining "…it was like, who cares about school when your life sucks? You know what I mean? Who cares?"

He was, however, able to survive both the tough neighborhood and the difficult family situation by making use of several talents at an early age. His use of "Restorative" enabled him to not only stay out of trouble but, at times, even stay alive. It also helped him deal with his alcoholic stepfather, who created turmoil on a daily basis and made his home life unstable. He also used the talent of "Includer"—being accepting of others—to deal with living in a neighborhood riddled with drugs, violence, and gangs. He recognized that being accepting of the other teens in the neighborhood and aligning himself with them would help him stay safe.

> My mind was on just being cool, being accepted. Because if you're in a neighborhood that's not the best and you're an outcast with the neighbors, you want to be accepted, you want to be a part of the crowd. So that's kind of what I did.

Jeremiah also exhibited the talent of "Responsibility" in maintaining the strong set of values that his mother gave him. As he put it:

> Raising us on her own, it was tough for her to always provide answers to the questions my brothers and I had. But she did instill in us a good foundation of morals, understanding, and respect. And when it came to our trying to accomplish whatever it was we wanted to do, she always told us to give everything we did a hundred percent effort, and to be proud of our accomplishments. If you do that, she said, it will make you successful.

THE HIGH SCHOOL ULTIMATUM

For Jeremiah, school was not a place to learn but rather a place where he could "hang out" with his friends, a result of his use of "Includer." Although he received what he describes as "decent" grades, peer pressure kept him from taking school seriously. That peer pressure, and the environment in the neighborhood, took precedence over his mother's efforts to keep him in school. Sensing school was becoming less and less important to her son, Jeremiah's mother would watch him leave for school everyday, not knowing that once he was out of view he changed direction and went to meet friends who were also ditching school.

When she learned, though, that Jeremiah had been cutting school on a regular basis, she gave him an ultimatum: Go to school or get a job. Having so little interest in school, Jeremiah's response was, "Well, I'm going to get a job." So two weeks before graduation, he left school and found the job pouring concrete. Looking at this decision from a long-term perspective, it's clear to Jeremiah that this was not the best choice he could have made. On the other hand, it does represent an example of his use of the talent of "Responsibility." Having seen his brother and many of his friends end up in prison, Jeremiah was determined to live his own life responsibly. For him that meant "busting his butt" for years in dead end jobs, trying to live by the values his mother gave him.

A LITTLE BIT OF A DREAM

Jeremiah was still working pouring concrete when, one day, driving to a job site, he passed a college campus. Watching the students walking around the campus, he saw a glimpse of a different life for himself. He had never seriously thought about college before, but seeing the students that day sparked his talent of "Futuristic," enabling him to envision what his future could be if he pursued a college degree.

> It was like a dream in a sense. The thought of attending college and excelling as a professional was something I had never anticipated for myself. The ability to dream about that being my actual life, and envisioning it mentally—all the benefits, the experiences, the opportunities—the whole fantasy about it being an actual reality, was something that kind of took me away. It was kind of like an escape from reality. And being able to keep the dream alive in my mind was something that provided peace, and allowed me to kind of deal with what was really in front of me. It gave me enough peace to make my reality more tolerable.

But Jeremiah didn't pursue the idea of going back to school, at least not at that point. He went on to get another job, this one working on automobile interiors. Like the earlier one, though, it paid very little and provided no opportunity for advancement. And one day, after a fight with his supervisor, he quit the job in frustration. Seeing an advertisement in the local paper for GED testing, it occurred to him that obtaining a diploma would improve his chances of finding a better job.

At first the whole reason for coming back [to education] was that I got tired of working for peanuts for people who didn't really care about me. I'd heard that school was a way to find a good job and actually get paid good money. That was the motivation.

But when Jeremiah received scores on the test that were high enough for him to get into college, staff members at the testing center encouraged him to enroll. Although he had dropped out of high school, he always did well in his classes. And now, at the age of twenty-eight, he discovered his talent of "Learner"—having a desire to learn and to continuously improve—as he embarked on a journey to learn something new. He explains:

When the lady [at the testing center] told me that she could help me get into school, I said that as long as I could get my foot in the door I'd be okay. I'd take off. Nothing was going to stop me from doing this. That was carved in stone. I knew that it was going to happen. The only thing that mattered was that I didn't mess it up. That was the most important thing to me.

COOL AND SURREAL

In his first semester at college Jeremiah took math, speech, and English composition classes at night and continued to work during the day. Although he was a little nervous in the speech class, since it was unlike anything he had taken in high school, overall he found the experience "cool" and "surreal," particularly when he reflected on the time he had passed a college campus some years before and tried to imagine himself as a student there.

After being a student for two years, Jeremiah considered college his "home away from home." He established close relationships with his instructors, and due to his academic success, was inducted into Phi Theta Kappa in the fall of 2007. Using his talent of "Includer," he also joined LULAC (League of United Latin American Citizens) in order to build a social network with people from similar backgrounds, and established new friendships with other students. At the same time, though, he began to encounter some difficulties in maintaining relationships with both those he met on campus and with his old friends.

In fact, several of his long-term relationships became strained almost as soon as Jeremiah enrolled in college. Some friends considered him a "traitor," or believed that he thought school had made him better than them. He even became reluctant to offer his opinion or speak out on some subjects because his old friends began accusing him of acting like he "knew it all." Much of this, of course, was due to the fact that his new friends generally had very different backgrounds than his old ones.

> Some of my old friends were affiliated with gangs. I hung out with people who carried guns, even when they went to school. I can remember times when they would even keep them in their lockers. It was pretty wild, but at the time I didn't really think anything about it. It was just the way it was. It was all kinds of crazy because some of my friends ended up going to prison, including one who killed a man. Growing up in that environment, I am surprised that I never got caught up in it to the point of no return. I was actually very lucky.

Reflecting on his past, he realized that he had become so different from many of his friends that in some cases he simply had to sever his ties to them.

> I had friends that I had known for twenty years. And it was like, I just couldn't be around them. You become what you hang out with eventually. And considering that I was trying to do something different, I realized that if I continually put myself in that situation the odds were that I was going to lose. I knew I had to do it, but it was tough to deal with.

In his remarks about the past Jeremiah exhibits several talents. Even though he struggled with the talent of "Includer" when dealing with his relationships, the talents of "Responsibility" and "Futuristic" helped him change his life by pursuing his college degree.

In fact, his talents provide an important illustration of the power of combination of talents. Without the combination of "Responsibility" and "Futuristic," Jeremiah's life may have ended up like so many of his friends.

Jeremiah now believes that college has unlocked a determination he did not previously know he had. Receiving a substantial scholarships, he transferred to a four-year institution in the fall of 2008, where he is now majoring in psychology and plans to continue his education through graduate school. Interestingly, even though he now sees a future of "living the good life," when asked where he sees himself he answers, "Trying to be someone. But it's like it still hasn't really hit me that I'm actually going to be a professional or something like that. It's still kind of scary."

THE ROLE OF TALENTS

The role of Jeremiah's talents of "Restorative," "Includer," "Responsibility," "Futuristic," and "Learner" are evident in his life journey. Early in his life, as a teenager, he made use of "Restorative," "Includer," and "Responsibility" to help him in his constant struggle with a tough neighborhood, a difficult family situation, and a peer group that had very different goals than he did. But he continued to use those talents later on in life as well, particularly "Responsibility," which enabled him to maintain the strong set of values he received from his mother, and to stay with unpleasant and low-paying jobs because he had agreed to work when he quit high school. Later on in life he also made use of both "Futuristic" and "Learner," the first when he saw a group of students on a college campus and was able to imagine himself in their position, and the second when he, at last, put himself in their position, and in the process discovered his desire to learn and improve himself.

How could drops of water know themselves to
be a river? Yet the river flows on.

-ANTOINE DE SAINT-EXUPERY

CHAPTER SIX

Dan

DELIBERATIVE-SIGNIFICANCE-RELATOR-COMPETITION-MAXIMIZER

Recovering from colon cancer at the age of thirty-six, Dan knew his life had been changed forever. For virtually his entire career he'd had jobs that were physically demanding, requiring him to work long hours as well as to do some manual labor. But the numerous surgeries he'd undergone had left him physically limited. The sole provider of his wife and three children, he did not want to rely on disability to support his family, but that meant redefining his career goals. Realizing that college was the answer, Dan decided to pursue a degree at the community college where he had taken classes years before. As he explains:

> I was a little scared because I didn't know how I was going to pay for things. But my mother was attending the college at the time, and she helped me out with some of the stuff. She told me to go to the Educational Opportunity Center to apply for financial aid. So the first semester was kind of painless as far as that kind of thing goes.

A LIFE'S JOURNEY

Dan, born in 1967, and self-identified as white, was raised in a family with an older sister and younger brother. His father didn't finish high school, and his mother had only an eighth grade education until she returned to school years later to receive her GED. The family owned a restaurant in a small community, and although Dan describes the family as middle class, he also says that money was tight. The family was by no means extravagant. New clothing was bought at the beginning of the school year, and expected to last until school started again the following year. The children also received very little for birthdays and Christmas. Even so, Dan remembers never going without. Although the family lived in a mid-sized community until Dan completed junior high, they moved to a smaller community when he started high school.

I THOUGHT IT WAS A JOKE

Academically, Dan never got "outstanding grades," and describes himself as "barely getting by." When asked what "barely getting by" meant, Dan says his grades were C's and D's. About his only motivation to get decent grades was to be eligible for sports. After being declared ineligible for basketball when he was in ninth grade, he connected with two teachers who were interested in helping him out. As he explains:

> The first semester I wasn't eligible because of a couple of D's, or an F or something. I started off my sophomore year with the same kind of grades, just sort of getting used to school, I guess. Then these two teachers helped me out. They didn't have to, but they did. They helped me get eligible for basketball, but with the stipulation that I had to do certain things or they would flunk me. That motivated me, and I turned it around. I went from C's and D's to A's and B's, and was on the honor role by my junior year.

This represents an early example of Dan's use of the talent of "Competition," that is, reveling in contests. The coaches clearly recognized this talent, and were willing to help him make use of it as a means of getting him to focus on academics. And it worked, enabling Dan to go from a C or D student to an A or B student.

Once he had experienced academic success, Dan decided that he wanted to attend a community college so he could pursue a career in teaching and coaching. But a couple of events occurred in his senior year that sidelined his plans for college. Arriving for class one day, Dan was sent to the principal's office for chewing gum, and was suspended from school for three days. He describes his reaction to the suspension:

> I thought it was a joke. I thought, "I can't believe this is happening to me." And my mom had the same reaction. Other than one time in junior high—when I pushed a kid because he was getting in a confrontation and he fell into another guy and broke his glasses—I'd never gotten into trouble in school. And over gum! My mom just thought it was ridiculous.

The second incident involved a teacher at the school. Someone had attempted to break into the teacher's house, and because he'd been concerned for his safety, the teacher had left the school. Several seniors and juniors joked that Dan was responsible for the attempted break-in. Shortly after, Dan was called into the superintendent's office and questioned about the incident by an officer from the State Police. He felt pressured by the school administration to quit school.

At the start of his junior year, Dan had a 3.52 grade point average. During his senior year, though, when he was questioned about the break-in at the teacher's house, his grades began to drop, graduating with a 2.0 grade point average. Although he did graduate from high school, he had, as he puts it, "a bad taste for school for quite a while," and instead of pursuing his dream of going to college he went straight to work.

THE GREATEST TEST

Disappointed and frustrated with his high school experience, Dan worked at a variety of jobs, each providing an increase in salary and responsibility over the previous one. After working on a farm and as a mechanic, he got a job at a Wendy's, where he eventually became an assistant manager earning $35,000 a year. After this position, he was hired in a sales/delivery position where he earned between $40,000 and $70,000 a year. Moving from one job to another in order to get ahead reflects Dan's use of several talents, including "Significance," that is, the desire to be important in the eyes of others; "Maximizer—focusing on strengths as a way to achieve personal excellence; and "Deliberative"—taking serious care in making decisions or choices. These talents provided Dan with not only the challenge he needed but also the motivation and direction to continually move forward in his career.

Dan's greatest test, however, came when he was diagnosed with colon cancer at the age of thirty-five. The sole support of his wife and three children, Dan knew he had to win the fight against cancer. He also knew that he was in for the fight of his life, and that his life would be different when the fight was over. As he explains:

> I had major stomach surgeries, and I knew there was no way I would be able to go back to the kind of work I'd done before I got sick. I can't lift things like I used to, because I'm afraid of getting a hernia, and the doctors agreed that I couldn't go back to a physical job. So I knew I had to do something else.

Using his talent of "Competition," Dan won his fight against cancer. And then, having beaten the disease, he once again tapped into his talents of "Significance," "Maximizer," and "Deliberative" to determine a new direction for his career. Realizing he could no longer work at a job that required long hours and manual labor, he understood that he needed a new direction that encompassed his desire for recognition, excellence, and careful decision making.

Receiving guidance from his mother, who was attending the community college herself at the time, Dan prepared to return to school. He describes the first day of class as "real scary." But even though he was concerned that he would be twice the age of most of his fellow students, he discovered that the campus was full of students from a broad range of ages and with a wide variety of experiences.

STAYING OUTSIDE THE BOX

The first four semesters were difficult for Dan. Still suffering from complications from his two major surgeries, he was ill at the end of every semester. Twice he ended up in the hospital, once during finals week. But despite the health issues that continued to plague him, his continuing use of "Competition," "Significance," and "Maximizer" enabled him to earn a cumulative grade point average of 3.3 in the first two years.

Like many others in his situation, he also developed a strong academic and social connection to the campus. Because Dan's new career goal required strong writing skills, he developed close relationships with both his English tutor and an English instructor who provided him with feedback on his papers. His other instructors also began to recognize him, although, as Dan says, " I don't know if that's a good thing or a bad thing."

In addition, he became socially active on campus, bringing his family to movie nights and getting involved in the formation of a new Student Support Services Club, of which he was subsequently elected president. The club, which coordinated various community service projects, also provided him with the "atta boy's" he felt were necessary, particularly for non-traditional students. In addition, his work with the club highlights another talent, "Relator," the ability to find deep satisfaction in working hard with friends to achieve a goal. As he explains, "Working with the club makes you understand that you're not alone, that there are other people who have gone through or are going through the same kind of thoughts and feelings that you are."

College also facilitated other changes in Dan. Besides his new career goal, he developed the goal of becoming a "more well-rounded person." He believes that people "get themselves in a box, and then they can't get out of it," so he now wants to "stay outside of the box." One way of doing that, he realized, was to take a variety of courses in different fields. As he explains:

> I wanted to get a degree in business. But I was also taking humanities and science courses, neither of which has anything to do with business. So they seemed like a big waste of time and money. But I understand now why taking courses like that makes a more well-rounded individual. It's not necessarily the subject but how you develop critical thinking that's the important thing.

Now Dan is looking forward to starting a foundation that will provide assistance to individuals who are undergoing a medical crisis. He sees the organization as supplying both financial assistance and other services, including crisis management, to those who need to focus on their health. As he explains, "When you're going through that kind of drama in your life, you don't think clearly." While this goal may seem very different from those he's had in the past, it's actually a continuation of his use of "Significance," "Maximizer, and "Deliberative."

> Where I'm going, where I am headed now, is still along the lines of being a teacher and coach. But instead of being a teacher of academics, I can be a teacher of life. I recently met a gal whose husband had just become disabled. And I realized from what she told me about her husband that when you become disabled you go through a grieving process just like you do when you lose anything else. And you know I'm going to be able to say, "Hey, I've gone through that and this is what I'm doing now." So I'm looking forward to a new life where I'll be able to live that, teach that, and coach other people on how to do it.

THE ROLE OF TALENTS

Dan's life journey reflects his use of the talents of "Competition," "Significance," "Maximizer," "Deliberative," and "Relator." "Competition" has played a particularly important role in his life, starting with his use of it in middle school. But once he graduated from high school and began working, he also started to make use of the talents of "Significance," "Maximizer," and "Deliberative" to continually increase his salary and level of responsibility. In addition, when faced with cancer, he again used "Competition," this time to help him weather his illness. Finally, finding himself in the position of having to refocus his career, he is using the talents of "Significance," "Maximizer," and "Deliberative" to start a foundation to help others who are faced with life-threatening illnesses.

You can often find in
rivers what you cannot find in oceans.

-INDIAN PROVERB

CHAPTER SEVEN

Corina

LEARNER-INCLUDER-RELATOR-RESPONSIBILITY-BELIEF

*C*orina was a senior in high school when she got pregnant with her son. She didn't want to quit school before she graduated, but feeling that she would have to stay home to care for her child after he was born, Corina was afraid that any hope she'd had for higher education was gone. Even so, not long afterward, she realized that having a child meant that her life was no longer just about herself, and that it would be important for her to be a role model for her son. As she puts it:

> I just want to set a good example for him, especially since he's a boy. I want to be able to help him as he's going to school, and I want him to be positive like me. If I can do it, then he can do it. I want to be just like my parents were, and encourage him the same way they encouraged me to go to college.

Having grown up in a family constantly struggling to make ends meet, Corina longed for a different future for her son. She believed higher education was necessary to provide for her family. As she says, "I always thought that if I went to college, I'd be a lot more financially stable than if I didn't." Having experienced a childhood of poverty, she learned to appreciate being able to have the basic things. And identifying her goal as building financial stability, she looked forward to a life in which "hopefully, one day, I wouldn't have to struggle for the little things that people don't appreciate."

A LIFE'S JOURNEY

Corina, self-identified as Hispanic, grew up in a home with both of her parents. She also has a brother, but as a child he lived down the street with their grandmother. Neither of her parents has a high school diploma: her father dropped out during high school, and her mother dropped out even before she started high school. Corina describes the family as "struggling a lot" financially. Because her father worked in construction, he was often unable to work due to the weather, and her mother couldn't work because of a work-related injury. Corina recalls that she received a lot of "hand-me-down" clothing from relatives, and that she got gifts for the holidays only sporadically. She also remembers that unless her parents were able to borrow money to buy school supplies, she simply went without. Unable due to their financial situation to purchase a home, her parents always rented houses in the community.

Growing up, Corina remembers one of those houses as being "really old," with cracks in the walls, and she recalls her mother putting pans all around the house when it rained because the roof leaked. And because the house had a heating stove rather than a furnace, the temperature ranged from "really, really hot to really, really cold." It was, as she describes it, "just a really ugly old house." Summarizing her parents' financial hardships, Corina says:

I saw how they struggled, and I didn't want to end up like that. I don't blame them for it, and I don't hate them. I realized that, even though they didn't succeed, they tried. It was just too hard for them.

YOU'RE SO SMART

Corina always believed that she was smart. As she recalls, even as a child, when she went shopping with her mother and grandmother, she would sit on the floor reading while they shopped. Her family reinforced her belief by telling her that "You're so smart," and "You have a good head on your shoulders." Her grandparents were particularly supportive, complimenting her frequently on her schoolwork. In fact, she recalls that when she told her grandparents that someday she would go to college they encouraged her, saying that she was indeed smart enough to accomplish that goal. Even as a young child, then, she demonstrated her use of the talent of "Learner"—having a desire to learn and continuously improve oneself. As she explains:

> I've always been the type to set a lot of goals and strive for the best grade I could, even if it wasn't an A. Just knowing that I tried really hard to earn the grades that I did made me feel good.

The only time Corina switched schools was as a sophomore in high school. Discussing her first school, she says that she "just didn't feel comfortable there." And she felt that the teachers there didn't care if she graduated. "I guess I was at the age where school didn't matter. I got off track and honestly needed motivation from a teacher or advisor to get me back on track. And that didn't happen at all." As a result, she had difficulty focusing on classes, and completed only four of the fifty credits required to graduate. This forced her to attend night school to catch up on required credits.

> High school wasn't hard. It was just having the self-discipline to gain fifty credits because to me that was a lot. It took me a while to realize how important graduation was for me. I always thought I wanted to go to college. I wanted to do better for myself, but I was always messing around.

Overall, transferring to a new high school was a good experience for Corina. For the first time in her life she got involved. Making use of the talent of "Includer"—being accepting of others, as well as of "Relator"—enjoying close relationships with others, she joined the school newspaper, honor societies, and LULAC (League of United Latin American Citizens). But she soon fell back into her old habits, began spending time with students who weren't very interested in school, and started cutting classes. Eventually the school's principal called her into his office to tell her that he couldn't see her graduating, and suggesting that she "stop wasting their time and just drop out." Rather than discouraging Corina, though, the interaction with the principal motivated her to complete high school. She stopped cutting classes, focused more on her work, and started seeking out the principal in the school's crowded hallways, making a point of speaking to him.

As her academic status improved, Corina was invited to participate in Talent Search, a program that helps provide both the information and skills first generation students need to successfully weather the college admissions process. She met regularly with her advisor from the program, got information about local four-year colleges, and went on campus visitation programs. The program helped her understand the academic as well as personal challenges connected to college, and she was looking forward to continuing her education once she graduated.

She also qualified for the school's honor roll, which meant a great deal to her. As she explains:

> They put the honor roll list on a wall at school, and I was so proud to have my name on it. At the same time my friends were saying, like, "Oh, all those people are geeks." So even though I was really happy that my name was up there, I didn't want to show it. My parents were really proud of me, though, particularly my dad. He was going around telling everybody that his daughter made the honor roll. Then they had this ceremony for all the people who got really good grades, and since you

could invite whoever you wanted, my parents came. The students who had a 4.00 GPA got a medal, and everyone else just got a certificate. And my dad said something like, "I'm really proud of you, and maybe next year you can get one of those medals." That did bring me down a little bit, I think, but I was really proud of myself anyway.

Then, during her senior year, Corina got pregnant with her son. Since the school's principal had earlier questioned her commitment to education, Corina worried about what he would think when he learned she was pregnant. As she describes her last few months in school:

I kind of didn't want him to know, because I didn't want him to think, well, yeah, she's definitely not going to make it now. But I started showing, so there was no way around it. Even so, when I graduated I made sure I shook his hand and looked him in the eye. I was, like, "You remember me, right? And he was, like, "Yes, I do, and I'm very proud of you."

After graduating from high school, Corina gave birth to her son. Exhibiting the talents of "Responsibility"—taking psychology ownership of what one says or does, and "Belief"—having core values that provide a defined purpose in life, she felt that she would have to stay home and take care of the baby for at least a few years. She soon came to realize, though, that college was the means to provide her son with a better life. Motivated primarily by that realization, and her desire for financial stability, Corina enrolled in college when her son was two-years-old. She explains:

I don't want to have to rent all my life like my parents have. I would love to get a house, a big house for my whole family, be able to pay all the bills, and still have money to enjoy other things. I always say I want to give them what I couldn't have growing up.

FINDING A PLACE TO FIT IN

Although Corina qualified for admission to a four-year institution, she chose to attend a local community college. Consistent with the talents of "Responsibility," "Includer," "Relator," and "Belief," Corina based her decision to attend a local community college on the cost of tuition and the belief that she would find others with similar roles and responsibilities.

> I guess I look at life at a four-year colleges as different from a community college. Like, I don't see a lot of students there having kids. Mostly they're there for school, but they party and go out, you know. They have that freedom, you know, of not being a parent. So it would be kind of awkward to be in a situation with so many people you can't relate to.

Corina receives financial aid to help pay for school, but since it doesn't provide financial support for her family, she has also had to work at a variety of part-time jobs, including one as a dietary aid at a nursing home. Again reflecting her use of "Responsibility," Corina explains the challenges of balancing work with school:

> Going to school and working part-time is really stressful. When I worked as a dietary aide it was at night, so I'd go to school in my work clothes because I had to go to work right after my classes were over. I'd get home about ten o'clock, sometimes as late as midnight, and I'd put my son to bed. Then I'd do my homework until about two or three in the morning, and I'd have to be at school the next day by nine. It was really hard.

At times, Corina feels like she is living in two different worlds—one at home and the other at school. Although she has the support of her parents to pursue a college degree, she sometimes feels that her mother does not understand the challenges of being a student. As she says, "Until I started college I didn't realize how my parents not having even graduated from high school made them who they are. When I talk to my mom I can tell that sometimes she just doesn't get it."

Enrolling in college has also changed Corina's relationship with her extended family. For example, although she grew up close to her cousins, she now feels that "we all kind of went our separate ways."

> There are certain things that I just can't talk to them about now because they're, like, "Okay, well, you're a nerd," or, "We don't get it." I don't want them to feel like I think I'm better or smarter than them because I'm going to college. They're really smart, and they're really cool, but we just don't see things the same way anymore.

If Corina has lost some of her connections with her family, she has developed new connections through school, particularly with the faculty. Because math is a challenging subject for her, she has had to work with tutors. But she describes feeling "really connected" with the tutors, and is very appreciative of their understanding of how hard she needs to work. And the hard work has paid off—up to this point she's earned a 3.4 grade point average. In addition, making use of her talents of "Includer" and "Relator," she has also joined several clubs and organizations, including LULAC, a bible study group, and the English Honor Society.

Corina has also noticed a difference in her relationships both in and out of school, and sometimes feels that she is caught between two different worlds:

> Going to college is a big change, and I was afraid that I would turn into a different person. I have a relative who went to college, and he acts so differently now. I don't want anyone to ever say that about me. I don't want my old friends to think that I think I am better than them because I'm in college, because I don't.

Looking to the future, Corina plans to transfer to a four-year institution to pursue a degree in either English or journalism, and would love to either teach or write for a magazine. She has considered graduate school, but is a little intimidated by the thought of spending more time in college. She does, however, think that pursuing a graduate degree "would be cool." Corina reflects on her college experience:

> I've struggled a lot in college. It's not that it's been hard, or that I didn't want to do it. It's just that a lot of things have happened that I've had to deal with. Like I lost my apartment, so I had to get a full-time job and couldn't finish one semester. I was also put on financial aid probation once. And then my grandmother passed away, which was really big for my family. And with all these things going on, it was hard for me to stay motivated to keep going to school. But I've realized that it's just what life is. You can't run away from it, but if you want to reach whatever goal you've set, you have to stay committed to it.

THE ROLE OF TALENTS

Corina's talents of "Learner," "Includer," "Relator," "Responsibility," and "Belief" are all evident in her life's journey. She first demonstrated he talent of "Learner" as a child, finding books to surround herself with during shopping trips with her mother and grandmother. Recognizing this talent, her family reinforced her love for learning by constantly telling Corina that she was smart. Later on, in high school, her talent of "Includer" became evident, as she struggled with feelings of not belonging. Transferring to a new school, she found a place to utilize her talents of "Relator" and "Includer," joining several clubs and organizations. And when she fell back into her old patterns of ditching school, she exhibited her talents of "Responsibility," "Learner," "Relator," and "Belief" when her principal challenged her to "stop wasting everyone's time and just drop out." Finally, even after graduating

74

from high school, Corina demonstrated her talents of "Includer," "Responsibility," "Learner," and Belief" as she pursued a degree at a local community, and continues to demonstrate it as she continues her education.

When the river is deepest,
it makes the least noise.

-PROVERB

CHAPTER EIGHT

Maverick

COMMUNICATION-INCLUDER-DEVELOPER-POSITIVITY-RESTORATIVE

*M*averick believes that the main lesson he's learned during his young life is not what to do but, rather, what not to do. Having watched his mother enter into a series of abusive relationships, and suffered both abusive stepfathers and homelessness at various times during his childhood because of it, Maverick longed for a different life. At the young age of fifteen, he decided the time was right to make a change. He not only moved out of his mother and stepfather's home, he also dropped out of high school, where he had experienced a great deal of pain and humiliation. Even so, before too much time had passed, he recognized that education was critical to a better future, and began completing a high school equivalency program through a local community college. As he explains:

> After seeing what life was like for my parents, who had not been
> to college, and the troubles that they dealt with, I developed a

desire and a need to go to college so I could make a better life for myself and, eventually, my children.

A Life's Journey

Maverick, age twenty and self-identified as white, describes his family as "a mother with three kids who kept choosing the wrong guys." His mother attended college for a period of time, but never graduated. He does not know his biological father's educational background because his father left the family when Maverick was very young, and the two were only recently reunited. The family had serious financial problems, at one point being homeless for two years. During this period, they stayed at shelters and, for an extended period of time, in a transitional house in their community.

When Maverick was ten his mother separated from one of his stepfathers, and the family moved into a condominium in what Maverick describes as "not a very good neighborhood." In fact, he, his mother, and his two siblings lived on about six thousand dollars a year, eating cereal and macaroni and cheese. He recalls witnessing two drug busts in the apartment next door, during one of which he opened the front door to see a police SWAT team on the front lawn. He also vividly remembers a woman hanging herself. Gang activity was common in the neighborhood, as was the sound of gunshots. Not surprisingly, all of this had an impact on him. As he describes it:

> I've always been paranoid because of the things that have happened. I'm also very aware of what's going on around me, and I've always paid attention to detail. Now, though, it's kind of nice, because I see some people who aren't street smart and I'm thankful that I am.

This comment is a good example of Maverick's use of the talents of "Positivity" and "Restorative." He exhibits "Positivity"—always being on the lookout for the positive in any situation, by being grateful for his street smarts, and "Restorative"—being able to deal effectively with problems, by developing confidence that he can handle any problems he may encounter on the streets.

ALWAYS IN TROUBLE

Because he moved within the community several times during his childhood, Maverick attended six or seven different elementary schools. This, combined with the lack of a stable home environment, led to difficulties in school. He recalls being "always in trouble and always the class clown," as a result of which, at one point, his teachers suspected he had ADHD or ADD. Finally, a principal at one of the elementary schools recognized that Maverick's behavior was due to boredom. He was placed in peak performance classes that kept him challenged through extra assignments that required more time and effort to complete.

Maverick had the most positive experience during middle school, partly because he remained in the same school for all three years, and partly because he and his friends competed for grades. As he remembers it, this was the first time in his life that he studied for school, and he received A's and B's in all his classes from sixth through eighth grade. Unfortunately, the positive attitude and environment of middle school did not extend to high school. Because there was a considerable amount of turmoil in his family life at the time, Maverick experienced great difficulty making the transition from middle to high school. There were a few teachers who seemed to truly care about his future, and made the extra effort to help, but those teachers were few and far between. More important, perhaps, he was beset by social problems. As he remembers:

> I had this extreme social anxiety. I'd get like panic attacks and freak out. I didn't like being in large crowds of people. I hated being in front of the class. I hated doing presentations. I think a lot of it was because of my past: my stepdad abusing me and my mom not believing me about it, and going from school to school, constantly meeting new people but never being able to open up to anyone. I just felt like there was no one I could trust.

These comments show how Maverick's inability to make use of his talents made high school such a difficult period for him. Although he had the talent of "Includer"—wanting to include others and make them feel a part of the group, Maverick felt like an outsider, and couldn't find the connection he longed for with his peers. He also had the talent of "Communication"—being able to put his thoughts into words, but his social anxiety disabled Maverick from communicating in the classroom, which led to additional pain and humiliation.

Finally, when Maverick was fifteen and in tenth grade, something happened in school that marked a turning point for him. As he explains:

One day, in front of the entire class, one of my teachers called my mom and told her that I was doing horribly, and that I was getting an F in the class. And I was so embarrassed by it that I just stopped going to that class.

At the same time, the situation at home was also deteriorating. Longing to escape, Maverick made the difficult choice to move out of his family's home:

Nothing at all was going good at the time. School wasn't going good. I wasn't getting along with my mom. I wasn't happy with where we lived. The house was horrible. I didn't want to live there at all. And then my best friend, my girlfriend's sister's boyfriend, told me that he had this low-life roommate who wasn't paying rent and was just freeloading, and asked me to move in.

But having moved out on his own, Maverick was faced with finding a way to support himself financially. After a couple of years of working full-time, first in a local department store, and then in an automotive dealership, he decided to complete high school through a diploma program at a local community college. It was while enrolled in that program that he attended a presentation on Fire Science, and decided he wanted to become a firefighter. So, recognizing that education was his path to a better future, once he had obtained his high school diploma, Maverick decided to pursue a degree in Fire Science at the same community college.

STRIVING FOR A BETTER LIFE

As Maverick began the enrollment process for college, he realized that he would need financial aid, and that he not only knew nothing about how to get it, he didn't even know what kind was available. With his mother's help, though, he figured it out, and now remembers crying the day he received the financial aid award letter because it meant that he would actually be able to attend school. As he remembers it:

> It was very important to me. I really wanted to strive to be better, and the cool thing was that I had a ton of friends around me when it happened. So we went out and had a really good time and celebrated. It was a really good night. I was totally relieved when I had the letter in my hands, because I didn't know if I could go to college until I got it.

This represents a good example of how Maverick made use of his talent of "Positivity," in this case being able to get others excited about what he was doing, which is evident in those who celebrate all life's successes and achievements.

Determined though he was to become a firefighter, Maverick had a difficult challenge to face while in pursuit of his degree: the mask that fight fighters wear during drills can trigger claustrophobia, and he had to find a way to overcome his fear. As he explains:

> They set us out in 85 degree weather, 90 degree weather, and they had us put on our masks. It was a competition to see who could last the longest breathing air through the mask. And even after you were off the air, you still had to sit there with your mask on and breathe through the hose. Some of those guys had been Marines, so they could breathe forever—they would not give up. It was really really hard, but I think I had that mask on for maybe two hours. I was freaking out and I

81

didn't think I was going to make it, but my will power, and my determination to be a firefighter and to prove to my instructors that I was there because I wanted to be there, kept me going.

This incident represents a good example of Maverick's use of several talents, including "Restorative," because he was energized by a problem, "Positivity," because it shows him celebrating an achievement, and "Developer"—recognizing and cultivating the potential of others, by his being part of an experiences that helps individuals grow.

Unfortunately, having dislocated his knee during his training in the Fire Science Program, Maverick was faced with a series of medical bills. In order to pay them off, for a period of almost two months he had to work as much as sixty-five hours a week while he attended school. Scheduling all his classes for two days each week, he spent the rest of his time working in a local department store and doing woodwork for a local construction company. But even though his schedule allowed for only four or five hours of sleep per night, Maverick was still able to maintain a 3.9 cumulative grade point average.

Maverick's use of the talents of "Restorative," "Positivity," and "Developer" continue to have a significant impact on the choices he makes. In deciding to work longer hours in order to pay off his medical bills, Maverick demonstrates his talent of "Restorative" by doing what needs to be done to solve his financial problems. In addition, even though he is getting only four or five hours of sleep a night, he exhibits "Positivity" by maintaining a positive attitude, and, in maintaining a 3.9 grade point average, demonstrates "Developer" by being committed to his own growth and development.

In the meantime, he has also developed strong academic and social connections on campus. His main academic connection is with the instructors in the Fire Science Department. Maverick attributes this connection to the structure of the program, with courses running from six in the morning to five in the afternoon three days a week. He also joined a study group for his EMT class, has used tutors for English, and has developed a strong connection to his academic advisor, admitting he would be "totally lost" without her.

Although Maverick's social connections are primarily with students in his classes, the most important one is probably with his mentor, whom he met through the Student Support Services Mentoring Program. As he explains:

> When I first met him we just went out to eat or just sat around and talked until we got comfortable with each other. He has a lot of experience in firefighting, and he taught me a lot about it. He also brought me to the local fire department and showed me around, and gave me my first taste of it. He was really encouraging, and very supportive. Later on, when I was looking for a part-time job, he introduced me to people at the fire station and arranged for me to do a shift. And I was hired the next week.

Maverick is very conscious of the impact enrolling in college had on his life. And perhaps not surprisingly, that impact has fostered his use of the talent of "Developer." He now encourages friends and family to pursue higher education, believing that it will help them reach their potential. As he explains:

> My best friend, who's been my friend for years, is the exact opposite of me. I pretty much forced him to go through the high school diploma program, but he still doesn't want to go to college. I haven't given up, though. I'm still trying to motivate him to go, so he can get out of the rut he's in.

But the most vivid illustration of Maverick's use of "Developer" is in his relationship with his younger brother and sister. "I just want to make sure they don't have to make the same mistakes I did. I want to make sure they get through school—high school. I pay them for every A they get, so they're pretty motivated."

Most important, he continues to be extremely motivated himself. As he says regarding his schooling:

> I think my experience of not having the best as a child, and then coming up through high school, choosing to leave, and then coming back, has made me a lot more thankful for the education. Having that break in time, where I didn't have any education, really helped me understand how important it is. So now that I'm in college and pursing my career, I'm completely motivated towards finishing my education and becoming a firefighter.

Maverick's attitude toward that education provides a good example of his use of both "Restorative" and "Positivity." He exhibits "Restorative" in solving the problems he experienced throughout his life by pursuing an education that will offer the stability he has always lacked. "Positivity" also plays an important role, helping him celebrate his successes while pursuing a career he respects and loves.

THE ROLE OF TALENTS

Maverick's use of the talents of "Restorative," "Positivity," "Developer," "Communication," and "Includer" has had a major impact on his life journey. Experiencing a difficult childhood, with an abusive stepfather and homelessness, he used a combination of "Restorative" and "Positivity" to survive. Acting as the class clown in elementary school, he demonstrated the talent of "Communication." Then, in high school, having been placed in an environment that lacked support for his talents of "Includer" and "Communication," his attitude toward school dramatically changed. And, finally, enrolling in college and deciding to pursue a career as a firefighter, Maverick found a goal that complemented his talents of "Restorative," "Positivity," "Developer," and "Includer."

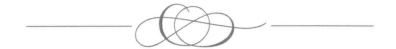

Sometimes if you stand on the bottom rail
of the bridge, and lean over to watch the
river slipping slowly away beneath you, you
will suddenly know everything there is to be
known.

–WINNIE THE POOH

CHAPTER NINE

Sheri

CONSISTENCY-HARMONY-LEARNER-ACHIEVER

For as long as she could remember, Sheri's goal was to get a college education. But having dropped out of school in the seventh grade, the likelihood of achieving that goal seemed remote at best. She never entirely gave up her dream, though, and at the age of twenty, already married and with two children, she took the first steps toward achieving it, getting a GED and then enrolling in a local community college to get a certificate in business. But her husband didn't want her to work, and although she did go back to work after they were divorced, she worked at a series of jobs with low pay and terrible working conditions just so she could support her family. Eventually she found herself working in a warehouse, and it was then that she reached a turning point. As she explains:

> The work was really hard on my body, and I was so tired I wanted to cry. I was also working with the meanest people, but I did it because I had kids. It just got worse and worse until, one day, I just couldn't take the job or the people anymore, and I

just walked out of there and said to myself, "I'm going back to school. I'm going to do it. I don't want any more jobs like this."

A LIFE'S JOURNEY

Sheri, self-identified as Hispanic, was brought up in a family with two older brothers and a younger sister. Her mother graduated from high school and wanted to continue to college, but never got the chance. Her father dropped out of school in the third or fourth grade and went to work in the fields to help his family. After he was married and had children, he worked as a contractor to support them, but in order for him to find work the family had to move frequently. In fact, during her childhood, Sheri lived in three different states—Montana, Colorado, and California, and changed neighborhoods, and schools, two to three times a year. She recalls never having school clothes or shoes, and celebrating Christmas only twice as a child. During a particularly difficult period of time, the family was reduced to living in the back of her father's truck. As she says:

> This is something I've only told a couple of people—that we were homeless. My dad made a camper out of wood in the back of the truck, and we would go and park somewhere at night and go to sleep. And then we would get up early and me and my sister would go into a gas station and wash our hair in the sink, put on our makeup for school, and stuff like that. And it was like that for a long time—a year or so. I hated it and I was embarrassed. And I'm sure that the people in town knew we were homeless. Sometimes, when dad had the money, we would stay in a hotel and take showers and things like that.

Being in such a situation would, of course, be difficult for anyone, but it was especially hard for Sheri because she has the talent of "Consistency"—valuing a stable environment in which everyone has the chance to show his or her worth. Unlike the other students we've seen, Sheri's constant moving, changing schools, and—especially—being homeless for a time, forced her to have to survive not only in a difficult environment but in one that was the exact opposite of what she needed most to flourish. And it's why, to this day, she has told only a handful of people that she experienced homelessness as a child.

Although Sheri does not recall any specific conversations about education, she believes her parents encouraged her and her siblings to go to school. Starting in sixth grade, though, she began "getting into trouble, making the wrong choices, and having the wrong friends," all of which created a difficult situation both at school and at home. She started seventh grade, but she never finished. Instead, she dropped out, and over the next several years continued to make a series of unfortunate choices.

The fact that Sheri also possesses the talent of "Harmony"—seeking to hold conflict and friction to a minimum—means that, as was the case with "Consistency," she was faced with a situation that was in direct opposition to one of her talents. Because she feels a heightened level of discomfort with conflict, when Sheri got into trouble at school the situation became so uncomfortable that her only choice was to leave. In fact, she still feels the pain of the choices she made during this period, and is very reluctant to discuss them.

By the time Sheri was in her early twenties, she was married and the mother of two. Realizing that without any further education she would be locked into a series of menial jobs, she decided to get a GED, and enrolled in a program at a local community college. As she explains:

> I wanted to do it for myself, because I knew that it was important. I hadn't accomplished anything in my life and that's something that I really wanted to accomplish. I was just so excited about it, so overwhelmed. I was really proud of myself, too, although I didn't share how happy I was with anyone. I guess that's kind of sad, but I was really was so happy.

Sheri's comments about getting a GED are a good example of her use of the talents of "Achiever"—taking great satisfaction from being busy and productive, and "Learner"—being drawn to the process of learning. Until she dropped out of school she had always done well, and she was excited about again being in an environment where she had the opportunity to learn. After obtaining her GED, Sheri decided to continue her education by enrolling in a business certificate program at the same community college. She recalls walking to school every day, regardless of the weather, determined to never miss class, an additional example of her use of the talents of "Achiever" and "Learner."

Although she had intended to go back to work after she received the certificate, her husband wanted her to stay at home with their children. It wasn't really what she wanted but, making use of the talent of "Harmony" to avoid conflict, she did as her husband asked. Even after she and her husband were divorced, however, and she went back to work, she took on a variety of relatively menial jobs to support her kids, including jobs at a local meatpacking company, cleaning houses, doing clerical work in a hospital, and, finally, in a warehouse. But returning to college was always in the back of her mind. And since she was now a single parent with three boys and a girl, she had even more motivation for completing her education. As she explains:

I mean, I don't want to be rich. I just want to be able to do something that I want to do, to be happy. To make enough money to support me and my kids and not have to feel like I'm in a bind all the time.

I JUST DUG IN THERE

Returning to the same community college where she had obtained her GED and business certificate, Sheri started her first semester determined to succeed. "I just went," she says. "I just dug in there. I was going to do it. And whatever it was, it was. And I'd go from there." She recalls that one of her first classes required research, and having no experience with research, her immediate reaction was to cry, convinced she needed to quit school. Instead, though, she persisted, and completed the semester. After that semester, and each succeeding one, she had an enormous sense of accomplishment, and became increasingly confident of her abilities as she continued her success in school. By the time she'd finished two years in college, she had earned a 3.06 cumulative grade point average. One term she even obtained a 3.75, after which she says:

> I didn't think I was smart enough. I didn't think I would be actually able to do it. I guess it's something that I wanted so bad that I just tried my hardest. I think I am smart enough to be here now.

Sheri's attitude toward her success in college is another good example of her use of the talents of "Achiever" and "Learner." She exhibited the use of "Achiever" in feeling a strong sense of accomplishment after successfully completing each semester, which in turn provided the motivation she needed to continue pursuing her degree. In addition, although Sheri always did well in school, dropping out in the seventh grade shook her confidence in her abilities to learn. Earning a series of strong GPA's, she began to realize that he could learn, and that she was indeed smart enough for college.

Like other students, Sheri has developed academic and social connections on the campus. She finds instructors approachable, and available for questions outside of the classroom. There are a few women in her classes close to her age, who are also returning after leaving school for a period of time, and they have become friends. She also takes her youngest children to family movie nights on campus.

College has changed Sheri in several ways. In addition to providing her with increased confidence, working toward completing her education has given her a great deal of pride in herself. She regrets leaving school at such a young age, but now she is sure that she will complete her degree. She has also gone from doubting she was smart enough to be in college to knowing that she is capable of achieving her goals. Five years into the future, Sheri pictures herself in a position in the accounting field. A long-term goal is to have her own business. She also hopes, of course, that her children will pursue college educations. The effect of all this on her new outlook on life is very clear.

> I guess it's because I'm happy and I look at things more positively. Just walking through the campus, I notice people more, I say "Hi" to more people, and I'm not as withdrawn. People know what you do. And I'm really proud of myself. I am.

THE ROLE OF TALENTS

Unlike other students we've seen, Sheri's possession of the innate talents of "Consistency," "Harmony," "Learner," and "Achiever" have to some extent made her life more rather than less difficult. Traveling around the country, changing schools often, and experiencing homelessness, Sheri lacked the type of environments necessary to make use of her talents, particularly those of "Consistency", "Learner," and Achiever." As a result, she rebelled in the seventh grade, and in the process inadvertently created an environment that was counter to her talent of "Harmony." Having herself caused trouble at school, Sheri struggled with the resulting tension of dealing with teachers and administrators, and eventually felt it necessary to drop out. It was only years later, after marrying, having children, getting divorced, and working at a series of difficult jobs, that she enrolled in a local community college and, at last, found an environment in which her talents would enable her to flourish.

If you dam a river it stagnates.
Running water is beautiful water.
So be a channel.

–ENGLISH PROVERB

CHAPTER TEN

Susan

ACHIEVER-RESPONSIBILITY-HARMONY-LEARNER-BELIEF

Susan was tired. For more than ten years she had worked hard tending bar to support her family, but at the age of twenty-nine she came to the realization that she didn't want to do that for the rest of her life. As she explains, "I didn't want to be that fifty-year-old woman still working the bar. I had to do something." That something was to enroll in a local community college to pursue a career in nursing. But she didn't only do it to change her own life, she also did it to change the lives of women in generations to come.

> I want to change this cycle of all of us getting married right out of high school, having kids, and never going any further with education. If I can make this change, maybe my kids won't follow in all of our paths, and they'll do something better with their lives.

A LIFE'S JOURNEY

Susan was born in Denver, Colorado. Self identified as white, her father left the family when she was three, so the only family she remembers are her mother and sister. "My mom was always working really hard, being a single mom," she says. "I remember being in daycare when I was younger. I love my mom. She was a great mom, and she was very responsible." Her mother worked as a beautician until back pain forced her to begin working at secretarial jobs. Struggling to keep the family afloat, Susan's mother did everything for her two daughters. "She would never buy anything for herself," Susan says. "We would have to make her." Despite having to struggle financially, Susan remembers always being happy, particularly at school.

I just remember being happy. I loved math, that was always fun. I loved band. I loved playing the trumpet. It was fun. A fun place to be. I loved school. I was never sick. I was the kind of kid who never faked being sick to get out of school because I loved going.

By recognizing the sacrifices her mother made to keep the family afloat, Lindsay demonstrates the talents of "Belief"—possessing core values that are unchanging, and "Responsibility"—taking ownership of what one says or does. Not surprisingly, she would subsequently exhibit the same talents in regard to her own children. Even as a child, though, her attitude toward school showed that she was already exhibiting the talents of "Achiever"—getting great satisfaction from being productive and busy, "Learner"—having a great desire to learn, and, again, "Responsibility," in this case through her involvement in school and the pure joy she experienced in learning.

When Susan was seven her mother remarried, and her biological father gave up his parental rights so that the girls' stepfather could adopt Susan and her sister. But their stepfather abused both of the girls, causing their mother to sink into a deep depression. "My mom was not available for a year," explains Susan. Her grandparents moved from California to Colorado to help the family through this difficult period. When Susan was ready for middle school, she was enrolled in a Christian private school. The school was small, with only twenty-eight students in her class, and uniforms were required. But because Susan's family had long been involved in—and committed to—religion, the environment was comfortable for her. And as she had always loved school, Susan settled easily into her new surroundings.

Everything seemed to go well through her first year in high school. As Susan explains:

In high school I became a cheerleader. I was, you know, that girl, whatever. That girl you wanted to be in high school. I worked so hard to be the only sophomore on the varsity squad. And I mean I loved cheerleading. I loved it. I remember wanting to go to college and be a college cheerleader.

Once she started tenth grade, though, things began to change.

In tenth grade, I messed up. I got a D in bible class, so I became ineligible for cheerleading. I had friends who were still on the cheerleading squad, but it was really weird. It changed everything about being there, and I just quit trying to do my best. And my mom said "Well, I'm not going to pay for you to attend private school if you're going to fail." But at that point I wanted to go to a public school, anyway, so I transferred. Pretty weird. That one D.

Having consistently focused on school and using her talents, Susan was devastated when she got the poor grade in bible class. Because she possessed the talent of "Belief," she had always trusted that persistence and hard work would pay off. And now, despite a lifetime of meeting her goals, she found herself struggling with the consequences of receiving a bad grade. Unfortunately, this one incident had a significant impact on Susan's future. This time, because neither hard work nor taking ownership of her actions were enough, she became disillusioned, and it changed the direction of her life.

The transition to public school marked the beginning of a period of rebellion for Susan. She began to argue with her mother about virtually everything, including wearing short shorts, which she'd never been able to do because of the strict dress code at the Christian school. "We just clashed," she says, "and it didn't end well for me." Since the public school she'd transferred to had less rigorous requirements for graduation, Susan took only two classes during her junior and senior years, and got a part-time job at Burger King. The job required her to work until midnight, though, and she had a lot of trouble getting up to go to class in the morning. Not surprisingly, her school work suffered. Even so, she continued working there, claiming "Once I get a job, I stick with it." In fact, part of the reason she stayed at Burger King was that it was a place where her talents of "Achiever," "Responsibility," and "Belief" were valued. Having not received this kind of positive reinforcement at school, she focused on work, and demonstrated her commitment by remaining on the job for two-and-a-half years. Continuing to argue with her mother, Susan's goal was to go on working and move out on her own immediately after graduation.

But since her mother wouldn't allow her to move out of the house until she was eighteen, Susan moved in with the parents of a high school friend for a couple of months. Then, shortly after her birthday, Susan found an apartment that she describes as "not the nicest place in the world," although it was all she could afford at the time. Her boss, who was in the process of getting out of a relationship at the time, shared the apartment with her, and she loved the freedom of being out from under her mother's supervision. She also changed jobs, working at a gas station sixty to eighty hours a week because, as she explains, "I wanted more money so I could go out and go dancing or whatever."

After three months of living on her own, Susan began dating her future husband. Two months after they met, she was pregnant with his child. Shortly after, the couple married and moved in together, and Susan began a new job at a jewelry store in a nearby mall. "I was excited. I always wanted to be a mom. I guess I thought that's what life was about. You know, you get married and you have babies." Her daughter was born in August, a little more than a year after she graduated from high school, and her mother's reaction was, according to Susan, "not good."

Susan was essentially the sole support of her young family, because her husband would work a job for a couple of weeks and then quit. "He'd always have like ten W-2s at the end of the year," she says. Fortunately, she enjoyed her work at the jewelry store, at least until she had a falling out with a co-worker and left to take another job in the mall. Shortly after, though, Susan discovered that she was pregnant again. Having a difficult time supporting the family on her salary, she, her husband, and their daughter moved in with her mother-in-law. But over time Susan got tired of holding the family together financially. As she explains:

> It frustrated me. I guess it was one of those things—just doing what I had to do for my kids. I'd watched my mom do it for us, and I'm proud that I did it too. But I got married because I wanted to be different from my mom. And here was my husband not doing anything while I went out to work every day. And then I came home one night and I had just had it, and I kicked him out.

The marriage had lasted three years, and after two years of separation the couple divorced. Susan's efforts to take care of her struggling family during this period represent additional examples of her making use of the talents of "Achiever," "Responsibility," and "Belief." Interestingly, they also show how she used the talent of "Harmony"—seeking areas of agreement—by avoiding conflict with her husband, despite being frustrated by his lengthy periods of unemployment.

After the divorce, Susan began working at a bar, where the money was good and she could support her kids. She also entered into a relationship with a co-worker in the bar which she describes as "incredible." When she got pregnant with her third child, the couple bought a house and moved in together. But then her boyfriend was diagnosed with Graves' Disease, which had a substantial impact on their relationship. The disease required the removal of his thyroid, which Susan describes as "medical hell." Because he became irritable and unable to work, Susan found herself returning to the role of sole support of the family.

> After a couple of years he was feeling better and he should have been able to get a job. But he had been out of work so long, and I was there to pay the bills, so he didn't. Granted, he stayed home and watched our daughter, but that was it. I just felt like he was capable of working, and watching me struggle should have been enough for him to get out and do something. But he didn't, and I felt like I was back where I was ten years ago.

It was then that Susan reached her turning point. For years she had watched her mother struggling to provide for her daughters, and she wanted her life to be different. So she broke off her relationship, and at the age of twenty-nine enrolled in a local community college, Because of her experience having children, she decided to pursue a career in nursing. "I love the whole process of delivery," she says. "I mean, it's a miracle. A life is born, and that's incredible."

The first semester of college was difficult for Susan. Although she had always worked in retailing, over time she had developed a high level of anxiety in public places. She believed that all those years of just working and taking care of her children had diminished her ability to feel comfortable in any type of social situation. Starting college classes heightened all those fears. Her first day of classes, as she recalls, she sat in the parking lot in tears, praying to "just give me the strength to get out of this car." When she did get out of the car, and began attending classes, she found that college renewed her love of learning:

> I love learning. I just love everything about it. I just like being able to know things. My mom was very street smart, but when it came to book smart, well, she hadn't gone to college. She got

married right out of high school. So when I needed help with my homework, she really couldn't help me. So it's nice to be able to help my kids, particularly because it's harder for them now, way harder than when I was in elementary school.

Although Susan can see a time when education will help her land a better paying, more fulfilling job, and her family won't be struggling, for now she continues to work very hard. A typical day consists of waking up at five-thirty to get her girls up for breakfast and get them ready for school. When her two older daughters head off to school, she drives the youngest one to daycare, then heads to her own school for a full day of classes. Several days a week she works at a bar, and on those days she drops the girls at their father's apartment, works until four in the morning, then gets a little sleep before her nine o'clock class. As she explains:

> As I tell my mom, I focus every day on where I'm trying to go. Because I have to go through all this if I want to get there. That's all that matters, getting through, taking it one day at a time. I've had to for my kids. They are what makes me do what I do. Like getting up after an hour-and-a-half of sleep to go to class. I know I have to do it no matter how much I don't want to. Otherwise, I probably would have just given up.

College offered Susan the opportunity to grow and develop by providing the best structure and opportunity for her to build a career. Entering the field of nursing would enable her to use her talents of "Achiever," "Responsibility," "Belief," "Learner," and "Harmony" in a productive, fulfilling way, while providing the means to support her family. Although Susan is still working long, difficult hours, now she is working toward a goal of building a better life for herself and her three daughters.

Susan's mother, as well as her ex-boyfriend, the father of her third daughter, have also been very helpful in enabling her to keep going when the going is very tough. On days when she is tired and doesn't want to go to class, they both push her to go.

Susan feels that the support she's getting from her mother is particularly meaningful, because her mother is painfully aware of the significance of completing a degree:

> Nobody's ever graduated from college in our family. And I know that when I graduate she'll be there crying. She just wants to see me make something of myself. She's watched me struggle for twelve years. She sees me following her and does not want that.

Through her struggles, Susan has noticed a change in the family. The conversation at the dinner table with her daughters often revolves around school. Even her four- year-old asks Susan what she did in school today.

> They ask me about my day, and they are just as excited as I am. They've seen me struggle. I don't want them to do the same. I always tell them how important education is, because more and more, as the years go by, you can't go anywhere in life without an education.

When asked what she believes to be her greatest success in college, Susan replies, "I made it to class." Upon further reflection, she continues:

> I find myself even speaking differently. I find myself not even using contractions any more because I am not allowed to in English Composition. It's really weird. It's sad because text messages become a whole lot longer when you don't use contractions. I use full words. School has also forced me to structure my life more because now I have more to do. When I wasn't in school, I just worked nights. That's it. Took care of the kids and worked. Now I am an organized person. It's definitely made me a whole lot more organized and structured. Like, my sister and I have to make an appointment two weeks in advance to get together because I've got everything timed out to the hour for two weeks in advance. And I've never been like that. But

now I have to. There were times when I would say, "I don't really feel like doing much today," and then not do it. But now even if don't feel like doing something, I still have to do it.

Looking down the road, Susan sees more college in her future after she's received her nursing degree. She is interested in continuing her education and wants to become a physician's assistant.

It would only take me another two years after I'm done here at community college. All my kids will be in school, so it's no big deal if I'm working nights as a nurse and going to school in the day, or vice versa. And who knows, right after that I'll have two out of the house and only one left with nothing left to do with my time. I don't know what I'll do then, maybe become a doctor!

For Susan, money has never been the primary reason for pursuing education. Nevertheless, looking at her future, she pictures a life without the financial struggles:

I have never been into personal possessions. I can't take them with me when I die. All I ever wanted was to provide the best I could for my kids. It doesn't have to be the best home as long as it's a nice home. It doesn't have to be the best car, as long as it can get me from point A to point B. We all look at those things, like, "Ooh, wouldn't that be nice," but I really don't care.

Susan's motivation has remained constant since enrolling in college: to carve a different path not only for herself but also for the women in her family. She envisions a future where they do not marry or have children at a young age, a future in which they don't have to go through the struggle she has endured throughout her life:

Our whole family history—we all do the same thing. Back in my great grandmother's time, it's what you did. But I just watched my mother struggle for so many years, and struggled myself the same way that she did. I don't want that life for my kids. And if I can be a better example—go to college and get my degree, even if I'm thirty and have a ten-year-old, if I can show them how to do it, then they will look at it in a more positive light. And, hopefully, they'll be able to do it at eighteen—and without the kids!

THE ROLE OF TALENTS

Susan's story demonstrates the use of her talents of "Achiever," "Responsibility," "Belief," "Learner," and "Harmony" throughout her life. Blending the first four talents, she was an exemplary student from kindergarten through ninth grade. Then, after struggling with a class in high school, the same talents led her away from school and toward working at a Burger King. Later on she made use of her talents to support her family, working countless hours while her husband remained unemployed for significant periods of time. During this period of her life she also made use of the talent of "Harmony" to maintain peace in the family, even though she was frustrated with receiving so little help or support from her husband. And when, after divorcing her husband, Susan entered into another relationship in which the same scenario occurred, she again used her talents to work long hours without the support of her boyfriend. Finally, coming to the realization that pursuing a career in nursing would help her support her family, Susan entered a community college where she can use all her talents to pursue a new career.

Follow the river and you will find the sea

-KING SOLOMAN

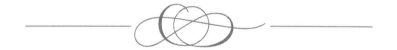

CHAPTER ELEVEN

Kimberly

RESTORATIVE- INPUT-BELIEF-RESPONSIBILITY

*T*imes were tough for Kimberly. At the age of twenty-one, having a difficult time making ends meet, she, her husband, and their two children lost their house and had no place to go. Then her husband left. "I don't think it was because he wanted to ditch us," explains Kimberly. "I think it was because he felt so bad about not being able to provide for us." Having no options, she and her two- and four-year-old sons had to move into a shelter. That spurred a realization for Kimberly:

I decided at that point that I wasn't going to ever rely on anybody again. And I wanted to get an education. I knew I was smart, and this was something I really wanted to go after.

Not long afterward, reunited with her husband and living in an apartment complex, Kimberly's goal remained unchanged. It was there that she met someone who encouraged her to enroll in the local community college.

> There was this girl at the apartment complex I lived in who was a student at the local university. Part of what happened was that she told me I shouldn't rely on my husband because of what had happened. But the other part was that I started helping her with her schoolwork. She was a senior in college, and I was sitting there, helping her do this. And she went, "Oh, my God, you're so smart. Why aren't you in school?" And that really boosted my confidence. She helped me do my FAFSA, and I went to the campus and applied. I was so nervous, so nervous. I had no idea where to even start.

A LIFE'S JOURNEY

Self-described as white, Kimberly was born in Texas and lived there, along with her brother and sister, for eight years. Her family moved often, rarely staying in one place for more than three to six months. Although, as she says, the moves were due to her parents' irresponsibility—both parents had substance abuse problems—"the good thing was that my grandparents always stayed in the same place, so we always had something like a home." Sometimes the family had no money for food, and they would have to go to her grandparents' home to eat.

Kimberly's parents were divorced when she was seven, but all three children continued to live with their father. A year later he remarried and moved the family to New Mexico. He stopped drinking, and for a while things were better. She attended school with her brother and sister, but she hated it, and often got into trouble. She describes times of fighting, being destructive, and being sent to the principal's office. After a year in New Mexico, the family moved again, this time to Tennessee.

But they only lived in Tennessee for a year before moving to Fort Collins, Colorado. Kimberly describes Fort Collins as being very different from the small towns she had lived in before. The schools were dramatically different as well—where she had been accustomed to classes of 15 students, she now found herself in classes with as many as thirty. With all that moving around, by the time she was ten-years-old she had attended five different elementary schools in five different cities.

Despite having changed schools so frequently, Kimberly always did well academically. Possessing what she describes as a "love for learning," she particularly enjoyed reading as well as writing. In fact, from a young age writing poetry became an outlet for her, enabling her to express her experiences and the challenges in her life through her poems. Unfortunately, academic success did not carry over to the social realm. After the family settled in Fort Collins, she often felt lonely and found it hard to fit in with the other students. As she explains:

> I just kind of kept to myself. I read a lot. I would sometimes hang out with other people, but I was never in the popular crowd or whatever. Especially because Fort Collins is kind of a yuppie town, and we were so poor. We were very different, you know.

But Kimberly's father's remarrying and moving the family from one place to another had other negative effects as well. As long as Kimberly had lived near her grandparents she could expect there to be at least some stability in her life. However, after her father remarried, her stepmother did not allow her to have any contact with either her grandparents or her mother. Feeling isolated, confused, and alone, Kimberly's life took a turn for the worse. Changing to a different elementary school in Fort Collins, she starting hanging out with kids she says were "not the best influence." She started shoplifting with one of her friends, and her stepmother discovered items that she and her friend had stolen from a store in the mall. Angry, her stepmother took Kimberly's books, music, and other things out of her room—she even removed the door—and would not allow Kimberly to talk to her friend again.

Now Kimberly's problems at home began to surface at school, and she became disrespectful to her teachers. "It was because I didn't know how to tell them what was going on at home," she explains. In the meantime, the issues between Kimberly and her stepmother continued to escalate.

> I remember I got a D in a some class like Home Economics. I couldn't stand the teacher, and she didn't like me. So again my stepmother took everything out of my room. I couldn't talk on the phone. I couldn't go out with my friends. Nothing. It was like that for two or three months. That's how long I was grounded for. She said it was because I talked back a lot. But I don't know.

Rather than improving, however, the environment at home became even more difficult. Kimberly's father and her stepmother fought all the time. Barred from contact with her mother and grandparents and, accordingly, lacking any stability in her home life, she became increasingly more depressed. At the age of twelve, Kimberly tried to commit suicide. "With all the stuff that I had gone through before, it was just too much."

Having experienced so much difficulty at such a young age, Kimberly was consistently using her talent of "Restorative"—being able to deal with problems—until the abundance of problems became too much for a twelve-year-old. For the next three years, Kimberly's life took a series of dramatic turns. Due to the severity of the situation, her life became one of pure survival.

After attempting suicide, she was placed in a treatment facility in Fort Collins. Although she was happy to be away from her family, she started getting into trouble in the facility. In fact, over the next three years, she was placed, and thrown out of six different facilities throughout the state. Her behavior might, however, be explained to some extent by two events that occurred during that period. The first was learning that her best friend had died in a car crash on a trip to Yellowstone. Kimberly had planned to go with her friend on that trip, and the news devastated her. The second event occurred three weeks before she was scheduled to be released from one of the facilities—her father and stepmother came to share the news that they were getting a divorce.

Her parents divorcing meant that she would have no suitable home environment to return to, and would have to spend another three months in the facility. Upset by the news that she would have to remain in the facility, Kimberly and another girl ran away, stole a car, and led police on a high speed chase. Because she was now fourteen, Kimberly became part of the juvenile legal system, and spent a week in a detention center before being sent back to the state facility.

Fortunately for Kimberly, the staff in the various facilities generally treated her differently than they did the other patients. "Everyone else was actually crazy," she says, "and the people who worked there could see that I wasn't." Even so, she spent several periods of time heavily medicated, sometimes being placed on three or four medications at the same time. During this period, her father rarely came to see her. Her mother, who had had no contact with her since she was seven, did visit once. "It was all my mother could do to not just take me and leave," Kimberly explains. "She knew what they were doing was wrong."

Although she had lived a lifetime of difficulty by the time she was fifteen, with the exception of her use of "Restorative," there is little evidence of Kimberly using any of her talents during this period. However, in addition to "Restorative," there are two other talents that most likely played some role in helping her get through the pain and trauma of spending three years in state hospitals. These are "Belief"—having certain core values that don't change, and "Input"—having a craving to know more. It was combining the talents of "Restorative" and "Belief" that helped Kimberly survive not only being hospitalized, but being constantly moved from one facility to another. And it was the talent of "Input" that provided her with an escape from the situation—reading just about anything she could find in order to know more about a host of different subjects.

Kimberly was just turning fifteen when she was finally released, having spent three years in six different state facilities. Her father and stepmother were divorced, so she came home to her father, brother, and sister. She completed her last quarter of junior high

111

school in the same school she'd left when she had gone to the first state facility.

> I was happy. I didn't have any problems fitting back into anything. I went right back to it. I got really good grades. But then we moved again, and that meant a new school. I actually started hanging out with some really bad people. I started getting into drugs and stuff. But I was doing good in school—I still got A's and B's.

Having occasionally drank and smoked pot in junior high, when Kimberly started high school her involvement in risky behaviors increased. She recalls meeting "bigger and better people"— by which she means people who had greater chemical dependencies, and spending entire days high on drugs and alcohol. Finally, having written what she describes as a "very horrible" letter to a school security guard, Kimberly was suspended from high school. Her grades were still good, but she nevertheless decided that it was time to drop out.

Her father wasn't home much during this period of time. He would leave for work at six o'clock in the morning, work all day, then be out until nine or ten o'clock at night, leaving Kimberly to care for her brother and sister. But rather than do so, she would hang out doing drugs with her friends. Kimberly describes the first time she used meth:

> It was actually with some friends I'd had for quite a while. They lived down the street from me. I always hung out with guys, never hung out with girls. I didn't like girls—they were annoying. I remember they were going to do some meth and they wanted to take me home 'cause they didn't want me to know what they were doing. But I caught on to what they were talking about, and I was, like, "I want to try." One of them was, like, "I don't think you should," and whatever. I told him that I could handle it. And I remember it was incredible. I can't explain it any other way. I did it five times, and I knew if I kept going I wouldn't stop.

But Kimberly did stop, and went back to school at a local alternative high school. Her return to education didn't last long, though—after she'd gone to school a few times she dropped out again. It was at this point that Kimberly met her future husband. She credits their starting to have a relationship with getting her off heavy drugs, although she still smoked pot. That relationship began as a friendship, but they soon started dating, and quickly decided they wanted to start a family. As Kimberly explains, "It was kind of an impulsive decision. I knew the reason I wanted to do it was because I wanted to give someone a better life than what I had. That's what it was."

Still involved in the juvenile legal system, Kimberly was tested regularly for drug use, and when several tests proved positive, she was sent to juvenile hall for two weeks while the courts considered committing her to another state facility for depression. But Kimberly decided she would not return to another state facility.

Whenever you are in there you have time to think. So I was, like, if that happens, I'm going to kill myself. I'm done. I had it all planned out and it would have worked. I knew it would have worked. I thought, "I can't keep living like this." And low and behold, three days before doomsday or whatever, I found out I was pregnant. So that changed my life around. I was in there for three months. I got my GED, I scored very high on it. I barely studied for the thing. And believe it or not, I was at college level on everything.

Testing extremely well on her GEDs gave Kimberly a new level of confidence. Although she'd had little formal education since junior high, she continued her own education while in various state facilities, reading all the time, particularly biographies. She also taught herself various skills, checking out books on various topics. Amidst all the difficulties in her life, Kimberly continued to learn.

Still pregnant when she was released from juvenile hall, Kimberly was sent to a foster home. Her foster parents encouraged her not to move back in with her father, believing he was not a good influence on her life. Kimberly stayed in foster care until her first son was born, but three months after his birth, she returned home to her father, brother, and sister.

Being at home with her family continued to be difficult, and Kimberly started looking for a way to move out on her own. She got a job at a Golden Corral, where she worked for about a month before starting to work at an Arby's. Having split up with her baby's father, Kimberly began a new relationship with a co-worker, and they moved in together. When their relationship ended, Kimberly re-united with her son's father.

It was at this point, at the age of eighteen, that Kimberly began to exhibit the talent of "Responsibility"—taking ownership of what one does or says—by deciding to return to school. She had completed all the necessary paperwork to go to college, and everything was set when she discovered she was pregnant with her second child. By this time, Kimberly had married the father of her children. But the family was broke, and although Kimberly tried to complete a certificate to become a Certified Nursing Assistant, she was unable to do it because of her pregnancy. The following year, when her second son was born, Kimberly decided to remain at home with her children for the next two years.

It was at the end of those two years that she met the college student who encouraged her to go back to school. But when she enrolled in a local community college, she says, she felt "clueless," and had no idea what classes to take. The most difficult aspect of school for Kimberly was the social aspect, largely because she had a hard time striking up conversations with new people. Gradually, though, she established some relationships that fit for her.

Academically, Kimberly found college interesting. Despite having little formal education since she had been twelve, Kimberly discovered that she had a passion for learning:

> I don't want to sound conceited or anything, but other people really struggle with school, and for me it's a piece of cake. I barely read any of my textbooks. I just kind of scanned them, and I did really well. I learned a lot already. The only thing I really had trouble with was writing, because I'd never written

a paper before in my life. But now that I have it down, I just love it.

During her first semester of college, Kimberly earned a 4.0 grade point average, an amazing accomplishment for a woman who'd received so little formal education. But college has created a new sense of empowerment for Kimberly. She now feels "a lot more grown up," able to pay the bills and take care of the kids. Looking towards the future, she plans to complete her associates degree, but is not sure of what type of career she will pursue. As she explains:

I don't know. I don't really want a typical job. I want to either change the world or just run away from it. People weren't meant to live this way. I know that. The world was not meant to be this way. That's not why it was created. There's no balance. Five years from now I could see myself going with the flow, doing what everybody else does and having a nice house, nice car, nice clothes. Or I could go and buy a little piece of land, and just live off it. One way or the other, I'm finally finding happiness. I know that. But it's a really weird feeling.

THE ROLE OF TALENTS

Having spent a life extraordinarily filled with turmoil, Kimberly was able to use her talents of "Restorative," "Input," "Belief," and "Responsibility" to help her survive. Although she made a series of choices that placed her in dangerous situations, her use of "Restorative" enabled her to deal with all the problems she encountered. Her use of "Input"—in this case reading everything she could lay her hands on—made it possible for her to escape the difficulties of her life, pass her GED, and eventually enroll in a community college. Exercising the talent of "Belief," Kimberly was able to enroll in college in order to provide her sons with the type of stability she'd never had in her own life. And, finally, using the talent of "Responsibility," she was able to build a better future for her family, and, for the first time, find happiness in her life.

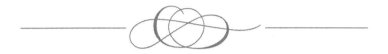

Eventually, all things merge into one,
and a river runs through it.

-NORMAN MACLEAN

CHAPTER TWELVE

Your Life as a River

*A*fter a journey full of twists and turns, turbulence and calm waters, the river nears the sea. Having started out as just a few drops of water, an amazing transformation has occurred. The river has now grown in size and force, forever changed by the path it has taken. Impacted by tributaries and streams along the way, the river shifted and changed directions a thousand different times and in a thousand different ways. But after traveling a great distance, the river has gained the strength needed to reach its final destination of the sea.

Each of us experiences a journey similar to the river's. We all gain size and strength as the years pass by. The difficult times and challenges of life are part of the journey, with each experience leaving an imprint on our lives. Sometimes the changes in direction leave us confused, and sometimes they enable us to see better how we can reach our desired destination. Our relationships are also critical to our lives' journeys, both the ones that come and go and those that last a lifetime. Although the nature of those relationships can be vastly different, like the changes we experience, the impact of each can change us forever. All of these things together—the changes in size and strength, the times of challenge and difficulty, the twists and turns on our path, and the relationships along the way—lead us to our life's destination.

Within each of us is a set of tools—our talents—which help us navigate the journey that is our life. Although these talents are always a factor in our journeys, many of us fail to understand how they can help us become the best versions of ourselves. But if you examine your life—your river—closely, not only does the role of your talents become clear, you can see how they offer the best possible path for your future.

If you were to draw your life as a river, what would you consider to be the key moments or turning points in your life? What about the times you experienced your greatest successes, or the moments that changed your life forever? How did you deal with the challenges that you faced? And who were the people that were important in your journey—family, friends, teachers, coaches, and bosses? If you drill down on each of these, you'll be able to see patterns of thoughts, feelings or behaviors—your talents—and how they helped you in times of challenge and success.

But how do you determine your unique talents? Each of the students profiled in this book did it by taking the Strengths Finder assessment, a tool designed to measure an individual's talents. The most effective method to identify your unique talents is to take this assessment. However, the descriptions of the thirty-four talents identified through the Strengths Finder assessment are listed in the appendix of this book. The descriptions provide a guide to help you identify your specific talents. So if you review the list, and think back on the events of your life, you will begin to recognize the patterns of behavior—the talents—that you have used.

The next step in the process is to examine your use of these talents in light of the four key aspects of your personal journey, as outlined in Chapter Two:

- The combination of your talents
- How you have used your talents in the balcony and basement

- How your talents have affected and been affected by your relationships
- How your talents have enabled you to survive the difficult times in your life

For each factor, what you will want to determine is how you have used your talents to create your greatest successes and overcome your most challenging experiences.

THE COMBINATION OF TALENTS

What truly makes each of us unique is how we use our combination of talents. If you were to reflect on the major successes in your life, what combination of talents contributed to your success? The combination could be two, three, or even all five of your talents. Whatever the particular blend, we all possess specific combinations that we continually draw on in certain situations.

Understanding your combination of talents begins with the examination of all your past successes. If you look at your record of success, a pattern of just how you use your combination of talents will emerge. We saw an example of how an individual continues to use a specific pattern of talents to achieve success in Susan's story. Beginning as a child, Susan used her talents of "Achiever," "Responsibility," "Learner," and "Belief" to be an exemplary student. Years later, after working long, difficult hours to support her family, Susan enrolled in a local community college so she could build a better life for herself and her three daughters. And when she did, she again used the same four talents to achieve academic success.

As the activities change, though, so can the combination of talents that you use. Early in his life, Maverick demonstrated a shift in the use of his talents between his home and school environments. In his efforts to deal with his turbulent childhood, Maverick used his talents of "Restorative" and "Positivity" to survive an abusive stepfather, homelessness, and violence in his neighborhood. In the classroom, though, the talents of "Communication" and "Includer" became critical as Maverick struggled to find his voice and place with peers at school. It's important for you to recognize the link between the type of activity and the combination of talents you use, because it will help you to begin any task with your best combination of talents in mind. In fact, building an awareness of your past successes with specific combinations of talents provides a roadmap for how to make the most of your talents in the future. Once you fully understand your patterns, you can define your goals with confidence, knowing the contribution your unique combination of talents can play in your success.

USING TALENTS IN THE BALCONY AND BASEMENT

Using our talents in positive, healthy ways—that is, using our talents in the balcony provides the opportunity for us to be our best. When our talents are being used in the balcony, we feel a lot of positive energy, and a high level of enthusiasm for accomplishing the task at hand. For example, by forging positive relationships with instructors, advisors, and peers as a student in a community college, Adriana demonstrated the balcony use of her talent of "Includer." In fact, the relationships she built were critical to her academic success because they provided the support and encouragement she needed to stay in school. No matter what the outcome, the boost we receive from partnering our talents with a complimentary activity feels right and natural, as though we are doing exactly what we were meant to do.

However, even when we use our talents in negative ways—that is, use our talents in the basement—we feel a similar kind of energy, because we are still engaged in an activity that uses our innate abilities. Returning to Adriana's story, we find an illustration of the basement use of the same talent of "Includer." During her junior high years, it was her use of "Includer" that facilitated her descent into a world of drugs. The difference, of course, is the purpose to which you are putting your talents, the specific type of activity, in this case something that was counter to Adriana's positive growth and development.

It's obviously to your advantage to keep you talents in the balcony, and the best way to do that is by watching out for the kind of things that can contribute to using your talents in counter-productive ways, such as the environment, your relationships, and certain types of activities. At one time or another you have probably found yourself in an environment that was unhealthy for you, such as a workplace where there wasn't a good fit between you and the combination of organizational values, tasks to be accomplished, and co-workers. We saw an example of this in Sheri's story, where her work environment and her co-workers created a workplace that was counter to her talent of "Harmony." As in Sheri's case, instead of bringing out your best, environments like these contribute to bringing out your worst. And your talents can make a situation like this even worse by making it difficult for you to see that the environment is counter to your growth and development. Environments can also stifle the use of your talents by making it impossible for you to tap into your natural abilities.

The same is true of relationships. Relationships can bring out our finest, enabling us to make the best use of our talents. But they can also encourage us to use our talents in unhealthy ways or inhibit the use of any talents at all. We saw, for example, how Sheri exhibited, at different times, both the balcony and basement use of the talent of "Harmony." She exhibited the balcony use in college by establishing good relationships with faculty, tutors, advisors, and students. But she exhibited the basement use by remaining for years in an abusive relationship with her ex-husband.

Finally, there are certain tasks or activities that can provide opportunities to be our very best or gravitate towards our worst. For example, Jeremiah demonstrated the use of the talent of "Restorative" by working in the field of automotive restoration, making the most of his ability to enhance car interiors. On the other hand, Jeremiah also used "Restorative"—by ditching school and using drugs—to stay safe in a crime-ridden neighborhood.

So as you think about your past, you should look for the best examples of the balcony use of your talents. Ask yourself what environment, relationships, and/or activities produced your best, or your worst. Look for patterns in the types of environments, relationships, and/or activities that tend to lead toward your using your talents in negative ways. Once you've determined these patterns, you can pursue certain factors necessary to create your balcony, using your talents to enhance your life. The most critical step is to understand what you need and what you should avoid to be not only your best, but to develop a healthy and productive use of your talents.

TALENTS AND RELATIONSHIPS

Beginning at the earliest stages of our lives, relationships are critical to our overall growth and development. But relationships also play an important role in how we use and develop our talents, both for good and ill. We've seen numerous examples of this. Mike's story provides a powerful example of the impact our relationships can have on our talents. Through most of his young life Mike's relationships with teachers led him away from school, eventually causing him to drop out at the age of fifteen. But it was also a relationship with a welding instructor that ultimately led to his enrolling in a local community college. The important thing to remember is that your use of talents is impacted by your relationships, one way or the other. In order to make sure that you use your talents to your best advantage in the future, you need to reflect on how your relationships have affected your use of talents in the past.

The first question you have to ask yourself is what you need in a relationship to ignite the use of your talents. Some people need relationships to be supportive, always encouraging them to do their best. Others find that their talents are brought out more often when their relationships challenge them, providing a dare to take on a task or activity. By reviewing your life, and thinking about what kind of relationships have most often affected the use of your talents, both positively and negatively, you will be able to get a better idea of the kind of relationships you need in order to grow and develop.

Imagine, for example, a nurse who possesses the talent of "Empathy"—that is, being able to sense the feelings of others. Someone like this would want to be able to use that talent to connect with people, particularly his or her patients. A good supervisor for this kind of person would be one who is supportive of this approach and encourages him or her to take the time necessary to connect with patients. If, instead, the supervisor is someone who has little tolerance for establishing these kinds of connections, the nurse is less likely to have the opportunity to exhibit his or her use of "Empathy."

On the other hand, a professional football player, who possesses the talent of "Competition"—needing to revel in contests and win, would most likely require a different approach. Someone like this would be able to make the best use of his talent by working with a coach who challenged him, an individual who could use the competitive nature of their relationship to challenge him to be his best.

So when you think about the moments in your life when you experienced your greatest successes, it's important that you ask yourself who was there with you, providing the spark you needed to ignite your talents. The nature of this relationship is critical for you to understand. Although the people in your life will change, if you want to achieve all you can, it is essential that you seek out the types of relationships that bring out the best in you and your talents.

USING TALENTS TO SURVIVE THE ROUGH TIMES

Your talents can serve as a resource during times of challenge and difficulty. Chances are you have already utilized your talents when times became tough. Understanding exactly how those talents can be an asset can provide you with the confidence you need to survive the difficult times we all experience in our lives. And the best way to start to attain that understanding is to think of an experience that you found to be particularly difficult.

In thinking about that experience, instead of concentrating on the turn of events, you should shift your focus to your patterns of thought, feelings or behaviors, that is, your talents (Clifton, Anderson and Schreiner 2006). What thoughts ran through your mind to help you sort out your next steps? How did you manage your feelings at the time so that you could deal with them effectively? And what behaviors did you utilize that enabled you to handle the situation? Let's say, for example, that you were diagnosed with a life-threatening illness. If you had the talent of "Strategic"—finding alternate ways to proceed, you would have been able to immediately determine all the options for treatment, weigh each option, and choose a path to follow. Similarly, if you had the talent of "Positivity"—possessing a tendency to be upbeat, you would have been able to remain hopeful, believing you had selected the best option for treatment and that you would overcome your illness. And if you had the talent of "Activator"—being busy and productive, you would have been better able to implement the actual steps you needed to move forward. The combination of these three talents, then, would have helped you determine the most appropriate steps to take, manage your emotions, and put the steps into action. Understanding how your particular talents surface during difficult times can provide a template you can use to manage challenges in the future.

Your talents are your key to building resilient behavior. Individuals with resilience can focus on their abilities during times of crisis, confident that they will be able to overcome whatever obstacles lie before them. It might be that one or more of your talents provides you with the ability to determine the cause of the problem. Or that they enable you to brainstorm a variety of solutions. Or that they can help you launch a strategy to solve your problem. Regardless of the specific role your talents might play, it is important for you to remember that it is only by examining the past that you will be able to determine how best to use your talents in the future.

FINAL THOUGHTS

Within each of us lies the potential to become the best version of ourselves. The set of tools that will guide us is our talents, the repeated patterns of thoughts, feelings, and behaviors that we have used throughout our lives. By examining our past, we can determine exactly how our talents have helped guide us through the various changes and challenges in our lives. Exploring the

Your Life as a River

four specific aspects of our talents (combination of talents, using positive and negative talents, relationships and talents, and using talents to get through hard times) will help us discover all the information we need to make the best use of our talents in the future.

Draw your river:

APPENDIX
Clifton Strengths Finder [1]
Definitions of Talents

Achiever   People especially talented in the Achiever theme have a great deal of stamina and work hard. They take great satisfaction from being busy and productive.

Activator   People especially talented in the Activator theme can make things happen by turning thoughts into action. They are often impatient.

Adaptability   People especially talented in the Adaptability theme prefer to "go with the flow." They tend to be "now" people who take things as they come and discover the future one day at a time.

Analytical   People especially talented in the Analytical theme search for reasons and causes. They have the ability to think about all the factors that might affect a situation.

Arranger   People especially talented in the Arranger theme can organize, but they also have a flexibility that complements this ability. They like to figure out how all of the pieces and resources can be arranged for maximum productivity.

Belief   People especially talented in the Belief theme have certain core values that are unchanging .Out of these values emerges a defined purpose for their life.

Command   People especially talented in the Command theme have presence. They can take control of a situation and make decisions.

Communication   People especially talented in the Communication theme generally find it easy to put their thoughts into words. They are good conversationalists and presenters.

Competition   People especially talented in the Competition theme measure their progress against the performance of others. They strive to win first place and revel in contests.

Connectedness   People especially talented in the Connectedness theme have faith in the links between all things. They believe there are few coincidences and that almost every event has a reason.

Consistency   People especially talented in the Consistency theme are keenly aware of the need to treat people the same. They try to treat everyone in the world with consistency by setting up clear rules and adhering to them.

Context   People especially talented in the Context theme enjoy thinking about the past. They understand the present by researching its history.

Deliberative   People especially talented in the Deliberative theme are best described by the serious care they take in making decisions or choices. They anticipate the obstacles.

Developer   People especially talented in the Developer theme recognize and cultivate the potential in others. They spot the signs of each small improvement and derive satisfaction from these improvements.

Discipline   People especially talented in the Discipline theme enjoy routine and structure. Their world is best described by the order they create.

Empathy   People especially talented in the Empathy theme can sense the feelings of other people by imagining themselves in others' lives or others' situations.

Focus   People especially talented in the Focus theme can take a direction, follow through and make the corrections necessary to stay on track. They prioritize, then act.

Futuristic   People especially talented in the Futuristic theme are inspired by the future and what could be. They inspire others with their visions of the future.

Harmony   People especially talented in the Harmony theme look for consensus. They don't enjoy conflict; rather, they seek areas of agreement.

Ideation　　　　People especially talented in the Ideation theme are fascinated by ideas. They are able to find connections between seemingly disparate phenomena.

Includer　　　　 People especially talented in the Includer theme are accepting of others. They show awareness of those who feel left out, and make an effort to include them.

Individualization　People especially talented in the Individualization theme are intrigued with the unique qualities of each person. They have a gift for figuring out how people who are different can work together productively.

Input　　　　　 People especially talented in the Input theme have a craving to know more. Often they like to collect and archive all kinds of information.

Intellection　　 People especially talented in the Intellection theme are characterized by their intellectual activity. They are introspective and appreciate intellectual discussions.

Learner　　　　 People especially talented in the Learner theme have a great desire to learn and want to continuously improve. In particular, the process of learning, rather than the outcome, excites them.

Maximizer　　　 People especially talented in the Maximizer theme focus on strengths as a way to stimulate personal and group excellence. They seek to transform something especially talented into something superb.

Positivity　　　 People especially talented in the Positivity theme have an enthusiasm that is contagious. They are upbeat and can get others excited about what they are going to do.

Relator　　　　 People who are especially talented in the Relator theme enjoy close relationships with others. They find deep satisfaction in working hard with friends to achieve a goal.

Responsibility　 People especially talented in the Responsibility theme take psychological ownership of what they say they will do. They are committed to stable values such as honesty and loyalty.

129

Restorative	People especially talented in the Restorative theme are adept at dealing with problems. They are good at figuring out what is wrong and resolving it.
Self-Assurance	People especially talented in the Self-Assurance theme feel confident in their ability to manage their own lives. They possess an inner compass that gives them confidence that their decisions are right.
Significance	People especially talented in the Significance theme want to be very important in the eyes of others. They are independent and want to be recognized.
Strategic	People especially talented in the Strategic theme create alternative ways to proceed. Faced with any given scenario, they can quickly spot the relevant patterns and issues.
Woo	People especially talented in the Woo theme love the challenge of meeting new people and winning them over. They derive satisfaction from breaking the ice and making a connection
End Note	The Clifton Strengths Finder definition of talents is provided/reprinted with the permission of the Gallup Organization

REFERENCES

Buckingham, Marcus and Donald O. Clifton. *Now, Discover Your Strengths.* New York: Free Press, 2001.

Clifton, D, E Anderson, and L. Schreiner. *Strength Quest.* New York: Gallup Press, 2006.

Erikson, Erik. *Idenity and the Life Cycle.* New York: International Universities Press, 1959.

19872317R00074

Made in the USA
Lexington, KY
10 January 2013